WOODCRAFT BASIC CONCEPTS AND SKILLS

OTHER BOOKS BY THE AUTHOR:

WOODCRAFT

BASIC CONCEPTS AND SKILLS **THELMA R. NEWMAN**

CHILTON BOOK COMPANY   RADNOR, PENNSYLVANIA

COPYRIGHT © 1976 BY THELMA R. NEWMAN
FIRST EDITION   ALL RIGHTS RESERVED
PUBLISHED IN RADNOR, PA., BY CHILTON BOOK COMPANY AND SIMUL-
TANEOUSLY IN DON MILLS, ONTARIO, CANADA, BY THOMAS NELSON &
SONS, LTD.

DESIGNED BY JEAN CALLAN KING/VISUALITY
MANUFACTURED IN THE UNITED STATES OF AMERICA

LIBRARY OF CONGRESS CATALOGING IN PUBLICATION DATA

NEWMAN, THELMA R
  WOODCRAFT: BASIC CONCEPTS AND SKILLS.

  (CHILTON'S CREATIVE CRAFTS SERIES)
  BIBLIOGRAPHY: P.
  INCLUDES INDEX.
  1. WOODWORK—AMATEURS' MANUALS.   I. TITLE.
TT185.N43 1976   684'.08   75-44325
ISBN 0-8019-6126-2
ISBN 0-8019-6127-0 PBK.

FRONT PANEL: BENT VENEER SCULPTURE BY BOB CISCELL; LAMI-
             NATED WOOD VENEER BARRETTES, EDWIN SPENCER;
             "WISHBONE" CHAIR BY ESPENET.
BACK PANEL: "NOAH'S ARK," THE ROCHESTER FOLK ART GUILD;
             LAMINATED VENEER NECKLACE BY EDWIN SPENCER;
             GIMSON CHAIR BY NEVILLE NEAL.

1234567890 5432109876

CONTENTS

ACKNOWLEDGMENTS ix
INTRODUCTION xi
LIST OF ILLUSTRATIONS xiii
LIST OF TABLES xvii

ABOUT WOOD 3
WHAT IS WOOD? 4
COMPOSITION OF THE TREE 4
CLASSIFICATION OF WOODS 6
SEASONING AND DRYING 8
LUMBER 9
CUTTING METHODS 9
GRADING WOODS 10
PURCHASING LUMBER 11
WOOD AS A THREE-DIMENSIONAL MATERIAL 11
COMMON WOODS: SOURCES, USES, AND CHARACTERISTICS 14

TOOLS AND EQUIPMENT 23
CUTTING INSTRUMENTS 24
WOODWORKING HANDSAWS 24
HAND-HELD MACHINE SAWS 26
STATIONARY MACHINE SAWS 27
SURFACE-CUTTING TOOLS 28
DRILLING AND BORING TOOLS 31
SANDING MACHINES 35
LATHES AND WOOD-TURNING TOOLS 37
MEASURING IMPLEMENTS 37
VISES AND CLAMPING TOOLS 38
ATTACHMENT AIDS 40

BASIC WOODWORKING OPERATIONS 41
PLANNING A FORM 42
DESIGN 42
CONTOURS AND TEMPLATES 43

FUNDAMENTAL SKILLS 43
CUTTING SHAPES 43
CURLING AND BENDING WOOD 45
JOINING AND GLUING WOOD 45
UTILIZING SCRAP PIECES 54
JOINTS THAT ARTICULATE 66
FINISHING TECHNIQUES 66
SANDING 68
TRANSPARENT STAINS 68
CLEAR FINISHES 75

4 BASIC CONSTRUCTION: MAKING A BOX 79
DESIGN AND MATERIALS 79
CONSTRUCTING THE PARTS 80
CUTTING 80
PLANING 84
FORMING JOINTS 84
CHAMFERING AND OILING 89
ASSEMBLING THE BOX 90
TONGUE AND GROOVE 90
FRAME AND PANEL 92
MAKING THE OPENING 93
FINISHING TOUCHES 93

5 TEXTURING AND CARVING 100
TEXTURING 100
WITH TOOLS 100
WITH HEAT AND FLAME 101
CARVING 105
BASIC PRINCIPLES 105
HOW TO BEGIN CARVING 108
LOW RELIEF CARVING 109
CHIP CARVING 112
HIGH RELIEF OR BAS RELIEF CARVING 115
OBJECTS THAT CAN BE CARVED 120

6 LAMINATION AND THREE-DIMENSIONAL CARVING 121
LAMINATING 121
ABOUT GLUES AND GLUING 122
TECHNIQUES 125
MAKING A BARRETTE 125
MAKING EARRINGS 129
WHITTLING OR HAND CARVING 130
DIRECT CARVING 134
CARVING WITH POWER TOOLS 147

7 | **TURNING WOOD ON A LATHE 152**
WOOD-TURNING EQUIPMENT 152
LATHES: TYPES AND CAPABILITIES 152
WOOD-TURNING TOOLS 153
OBJECTS THAT CAN BE MADE BY TURNING 158
SPINDLE TURNING 158
ATTACHING WOOD TO LATHE 158
CUTTING AND SCRAPING 158
FACEPLATE TURNING 162
PREPARATION 162
TURNING THE FORM 162
FINISHING 168

8 | **THE BASICS OF MAKING A CHAIR 182**
CONSTRUCTION PLAN 182
JOINTS 184
MATERIALS 186
FORMING PARTS 186
BENDING BACK SLATS 186
SHAPING RAILS, LEGS, OR SLATS 189
TURNING SPINDLES, LEGS, OR RAILS 190
ASSEMBLING PARTS 190
FINISHING 192
RUSH WORK 194

9 | **MAKING A BASIC CABINET 198**
PLANNING THE CABINET 198
DESIGN CONSIDERATIONS 198
TYPES OF CONSTRUCTION 199
MATERIALS 199
JOINTS 199
MAKING THE PARTS 200
CUTTING THE LUMBER 200
FORMING JOINTS 200
FITTINGS 207
ASSEMBLING COMPONENTS 208
PRELIMINARY CHECKING 208
THE CARCASS AND BACK PANEL 210
DIVIDERS AND DRAWERS 211
ACCESSORIES 211

GLOSSARY 218
SOURCES OF SUPPLY 221
BIBLIOGRAPHY 225
INDEX 227

ACKNOWLEDGMENTS

It is a fact that, without the contributions of first-rate work by artist-craftsmen from all over the world, this book could not have been written. Among these people, I owe very special thanks to Joyce and Edgar Anderson, Edwin Spencer, Ron Roszkiewicz, Robert Sperber, Peter Child, and Neville Neal.

Very special thanks go to my sons Jay and Lee Newman who pitched in in countless ways, along with my husband Jack, my Quartermaster-General. My debt to them is greatest.

Deep appreciation is also reserved for Norm Smith for his first-rate photo processing and for Patricia Weidner for her behind-the-typewriter assistance.

Woodworking has consistently been one of the most popular creative hobbies in the world. There is good reason, because there is a genuine sense of accomplishment in working with wood—cutting, shaping, fitting, assembling something of one's own design. And there is a continuing pleasure when the piece functions as an attribute to living.

This book was organized and structured through the author's consideration of basic concepts and skills used in woodworking. This should provide a sound foundation for the beginner and intermediate level woodworker. And of course, it is hoped that the quality of design shown within, with its dominant leaning toward basic, simple, essential form, will inspire the woodworker as well.

Included are tables, finely detailed photographic sequences showing how to go about performing woodworking operations, as well as a glossary, sources of supply list, and a suggested reading list. Learning goes on because woodworking is one field where one cannot know enough. Content is vast. Perhaps the material within this book will provide the motivation to continue learning and creating. Instructions, though, can suffice in order for one to create similar forms. As in any area where patience, good sense, knowledge, and skill are attributes, one must practice to achieve proficiency.

Wood, in the long run, will continue to be with us, as it has always been, and will provide abundant pleasure—to look at and to utilize and to use as a creative material.

FIGURE

1.1 Microscopic thin sections
of hardwood and softwood   5
1.2 Cross section of loblolly pine
tree   6
1.3 Examples of wood types   7
1.4 Seasoning wood   8
1.5 How a tree is used   10
1.6 Old wooden beehive   12
1.7 Hand-carved platter   13
1.8 Pine and mahogany chess set   13

FIGURE

2.1 Hand saws   25
2.2 Miter box and back saw   26
2.3 Saber saw   27
2.4 Scroll saw   28
2.5 Wood-trimming planes   29
2.6 Woodcarving tools   30
2.7 Surform tools   31
2.8 Cutting tools   32
2.9 Bits and bores   33
2.10 Ratchet and bits   34
2.11 Electric hand drill and
accessories   35
2.12 Electric sander   36
2.13 Disk sander   36
2.14 Measuring devices   38
2.15 Clamps   39
2.16 Hammering tools   40
2.17 Pliers and screwdrivers   40

FIGURE

3.1 Using a marking gauge   44
3.2 Using dividers   44
3.3 Technique for using crosscut
saw   45
3.4 Using a coping saw   46
3.5 Using a back saw in a miter box   47
3.6 Using a scroll saw or jigsaw   48
3.7 Using a band saw with a fence
or jig   49
3.8 Using a table saw   49
3.9 Pushers used with table saw   50
3.10 Using a drill press   50
3.11 Cutting internal patterns with a
router bit   51

3.12 Finishing on a rotating sanding
drum   51
3.13 Procedures in making a jigsaw
puzzle   52
3.14 Three-dimensional puzzle
sculpture   53
3.15 Puzzle painting in wood   54
3.16 Keyboard and wooden disks   55
3.17 Cube pencil holder   55
3.18 Mirror framed in wood   56
3.19 Procedure for sculpturing with
veneer   56, 57
3.20 Steps in making a veneer
butterfly   57–59
3.21 Japanese holiday ornament   60
3.22 Finnish flowers made from pine
shavings   61
3.23 Closeup of pine flowers   62
3.24 Common joints used to attach
wood parts   63
3.25 Utilizing cross lap joints to make
a trivet   64–66
3.26 A trivet made from cross sections
of birch   67
3.27 A butter box made of birch bark
and wood   68
3.28 Interior of the butter box   68
3.29 Handmade Swedish hangers   69
3.30 Wine rack   70
3.31 "Noah's Ark," oak and cedar with
maple figurines   71
3.32 Making a lamp from scrap pieces
of walnut   71–73
3.33 "16 Balls, 16 Cubes on
7 Shelves"   74
3.34 A wood relief made from pine
scraps   75
3.35 Making a toy with movable
joints   76, 77
3.36 Toys made of laminated pine   77

FIGURE

4.1 Cutting and planing wood to
dimension for a box   81–83
4.2 Making dovetail joints for
joining the box   84–87
4.3 Forming tongue and groove to fit
panels into frame   88

4.4 Sanding and chamfering parts 89
4.5 Oiling parts before assembly 90
4.6 Forming a tongue on the shaper-cutter 91
4.7 Attaching dividers in box 92
4.8 Assembling the box and separating the lid 93, 94
4.9 Attaching hinges to the box 95, 96
4.10 Finishing the surfaces 97
4.11 Interior of completed box 98
4.12 Box exterior, walnut and butternut hickory 98
4.13 Unique walnut-topped box 99

FIGURE

5.1 Flame-textured Japanese tray 101
5.2 Burning in a decorative design 103, 104
5.3 Boxes from Poland with burned-in designs 105
5.4 Box interior displays joints 106
5.5 Heat-decorated and painted elements 106
5.6 Cutting board with burned-in accents 107
5.7 Basic carving cuts 107
5.8 Tool cutting edges in cross section 110
5.9 Making an inlayed and carved wooden plaque 111, 112
5.10 Shallow carved decorative plate 113
5.11 Shallow carved Thai box 114
5.12 Box surfaces incised and carved in shallow relief 114
5.13 Chip carving strokes 115
5.14 Eighteenth-century Dutch mangle boards 116
5.15 Chip carving and incise carving 117
5.16 Yugoslavian box with chip carving 118
5.17 Chip carved peasant's wooden spoon 118
5.18 High relief carving in Ohrid Debar style 119
5.19 Contemporary high relief carving 120

FIGURE

6.1 Solid wood cubes and cylinders 122
6.2 Lamp with butcher block base 123
6.3 Plywood sculpture 124
6.4 Making a barrette from laminated veneers 126–128
6.5 Rough and refined earring forms 129
6.6 Making earrings from laminated and rolled veneers 129, 130
6.7 Laminated earrings 131
6.8 Necklace made from laminated wood 132
6.9 Two pendant necklaces 133
6.10 Bracelet strung on elastic 133
6.11 Ring forms from laminated veneers 134
6.12 Tanzanian man whittling a wooden sculpture 135
6.13 Whittled sculpture from the Ivory Coast 136
6.14 Whittling figurines from wood thorns 137, 138
6.15 Another thorn carving 138
6.16 Mexican figurines whittled from softwood 139
6.17 Symbolic forms whittled by Cuna Indians 139
6.18 Decorative whittled forms from Japan 140
6.19 Carving a sculpture from a solid wood block 140–142
6.20 Making a template 143
6.21 Carving green wood with an adz 143, 144
6.22 "Frog Haven," a jewelry box 144
6.23 Another view of jewelry box 145
6.24 A wooden hand, carved to hold a mirror 145
6.25 Wood door knocker with inlaid eyes 146
6.26 Richly textured mirror frame 147
6.27 Textured pendants 148
6.28 Carved rings 148
6.29 African mahogany bowl 149
6.30 Carved walnut bowl 149

6.31 "Pony Tail," a highly textured sculpture 150

6.32 Moto-Tool for power carving 151

FIGURE

7.1 Moto-Lathe for small hobby work 153

7.2 Wood-turning lathe 154

7.3 Wood-turning tools 155

7.4 Procedure for sharpening tools 156, 157

7.5 Making a cylindrical form by spindle turning 159, 160

7.6 Spindle turned lamp base 161

7.7 Turning a wood bowl using faceplate method 162–167

7.8 A bowl formed by faceplate turning 168

7.9 Making a cylindrical box and lid by faceplate turning 169–175

7.10 Wood forms 176

7.11 Turned wood forms 176

7.12 Forms turned on a lathe 177

7.13 Turned bowl of Mexican mahogany 177

7.14 A variety of turned forms 178

7.15 Large, flat platter 179

7.16 Turned cups and platter 179

7.17 Teak and walnut vases 180

7.18 Plate and chalice 181

FIGURE

8.1 Basic Gimson chair 183

8.2 Ladder-backed Gimsons 184

8.3 Spindle-backed rocking chair 185

8.4 Storing roughly cut parts 186

8.5 Boiling and bending wood for slats 187, 188

8.6 Shaping and surfacing chair rails and legs 189, 190

8.7 Spindle turning wood strips for chair legs and spindles 191, 192

8.8 Parts are assembled and clamped 193

8.9 Rush work for chair seating 194, 195

8.10 Hand-carved walnut chair 196

8.11 Another view of walnut chair 197

FIGURE

9.1 Cutting lumber to dimensions for cabinet 200, 201

9.2 Making the dovetail joints 201–204

9.3 Cutting mortise joints for the spline 204, 205

9.4 Making lap joints in back panel frame 206, 207

9.5 Making half-blind dovetail joints for drawers 208

9.6 Making and fitting drawer rails into carcass 209

9.7 Assembling carcass and back panel 210, 211

9.8 Accessories ready for attachment 212

9.9 Attaching handmade wooden hinges 212

9.10 Affixing wood latch 213

9.11 Chamfering and planing drawers for fit 213

9.12 Natural grain of hickory wood shows in cabinet door 214

9.13 Interior of the jewelry cabinet 215

9.14 Insets for hanging the cabinet 216

9.15 Detail view of cabinet bottom 217

LIST OF COLOR ILLUSTRATIONS

Figure

1 Three-dimensional puzzle sculpture
2 Laminated wood veneer barrettes
3 Storage unit of Siamese padouk
4 Veneer sculpture
5 Bulgarian box with burned-in design
6 "Wishbone" chair
7 Carved jewelry box
8 Faceplate turned trays
9 Laminated veneer necklace
10 Jigsaw picture puzzle
11 Scandinavian veneer flowers
12 Liquor storage unit
13 Carved Hungarian box
14 Spindle turned vase forms
15 Carved, flame-textured tray
16 Bubinga and ebony stool

LIST OF TABLES

Table

A Comparative Ease of Working with Hand Tools   18
B Comparative Ease of Planing Hardwoods   19
C Comparative Toughness   19
D Relative Hardness   20
E Comparative Freedom from Warping   20
F Tendency of Woods to Shrink and Swell   21
G Retention of Odor and Taste When Dry   21
H Comparative Amount of Figure in Woods   22
I Suggested Lathe Speeds   154
J Relative Yield of Smooth Turnings in Percentages   155
K Comparative Bending Breakage of Hardwoods   188

WOODCRAFT BASIC CONCEPTS AND SKILLS

ABOUT WOOD

Wood was one of the earliest materials used by man. It became his weapon, tool, implement, fuel, shelter, container, furniture, and even his clothing. People learned that wood was pleasing and warm to touch (it could be smooth or rough), yet it was a poor conductor of heat. They learned that wood could be strong, yet elastic and bendable. They discovered that edges of wooden implements would not cut flesh when handled; yet, wood was rigid and dense enough to be fashioned into arrows and knives. On the other hand, although wood was soft enough to be cut and shaped with simple hand tools, it was impenetrable enough to be hewn into protective portable shields that could deflect blows of weapons. Because wood was strong and lightweight and easy to form, it became a significant building material portable enough to be brought to a site and worked there. Wood also became a source material for the making of other products such as paper, and later became a source of chemical components for all kinds of materials.

No part of a tree was unusable. The tree provided foods such as fruits and nuts. It was the source of medicines and poisons. Some seeds were used as soaps, others as dyes. Leaves that were rough functioned as sandpapers. Leaves that were smooth and waxy became wrappings or packages for foods that were cooked directly over hot coals. Other leaves served as thatching for roofs. Vines from the tree were twisted into roving for fences; its bark was steeped as tanning agents for leather. Its ashes were mixed as glazes for pottery. Its saps became syrups, adhesives and paint thinners.

The tree was the refresher of the air; its roots kept soil from eroding; its foliage mulched and replenished the soil, as well as serving as an umbrella and screen from the sun, rain, and wind. The tree has been both beautiful and bountiful. And in most places of the world, wood has been plentiful and relatively cheap. Unlike other resources of the earth, the supply of wood is replaceable—over the long run.

WHAT IS WOOD?

People learned that all wood is basically similar, yet that each species is very different and unique. They learned that wood from one tree had different characteristics, and therefore different uses, than wood from another tree. People closely examined the structure of wood and saw differences. They perceived that ash was threaded throughout with large pores, set in distinct rings which alternated with rings that were quite different: strong, hard, heavy summerwood. This was why ash was strong and elastic, and would not split when subjected to repeated blows and hard shocks. So they fashioned ash into handles for their stone axes. To this day, ash wood is used as tool and implement handles. They learned that elm was difficult to split, so they utilized it in making chair seats; that oak proved to be slow to decay, so it was chosen for fence posts and for the structural elements of buildings. Over the centuries the qualities and uses for wood became part of the woodworker's lore.

Composition of the Tree A microscopic examination will show that wood is made up of bundles of fibers or long tubular cells that are cemented together solidly by wood's own adhesive, lignin (Fig. 1.1). These tubular cells are the plumbing system of the tree. This is the grain that you see on surfaces and edges, the cells that run parallel to the stem of the tree. These tubular cells are crossed by other fibers that form the medullary or wood rays. These function as the passageways for nourishment which feeds the tree. They are seen as the wood rays that pass from the center, or pith, of the tree to the bark. They serve also to bind units together.

As we look at the cross section of a tree trunk in Figure 1.2, we can see concentric rings. These rings are formed as a layer of wood for each year of a tree's life. That is why they are referred to as "annual rings." At the center of the cross section is the pith, which is lighter in color and less strong. Next is the heartwood, which lies between the pith and the sapwood. The heartwood, which is made up of older, dead layers, is the strongest wood section of the tree and helps it to remain straight and upright. Sapwood layers come next and consist of the most recent annual rings, new wood lying between the heartwood and cambium. Sapwood, the tree's pipeline for water moving up to the leaves, is softer than heartwood and yet harder than the cambium, which is the most recent annual ring. The cambium consists of a two-celled layer: one thin layer is the inner bark called *bast* or *phloem.* The next thin layer is the part that grows, producing new bark on the side away from the pith and new sapwood on the side toward the pith. Sap, the food made in the leaves, is carried downward through the bast to feed branches, trunk, and roots. Finally, there is the outer bark which is the external protective layer of the tree, continually renewed from within. It helps the tree to retain its moisture, insulates against heat and cold, and wards off insect enemies.

Growth of wood is affected by various environmental conditions—seasons, moisture, sunlight, insects. As a matter of fact, even after wood has been chopped down, it continues to react to environmental conditions. And almost the same elements will affect it—moisture, heat, and insects. As we look at a

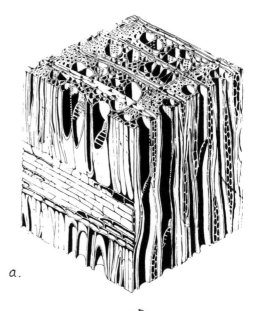

a.

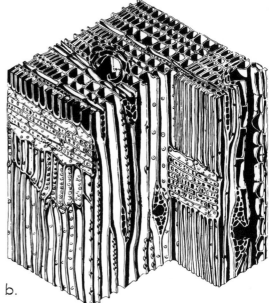

b.

Fig. 1.1 A diagram based on a microscopic view of a thin section of hardwood (a) and softwood (b). The block actually measured about ¼ inch on a side. Under the microscope, one can see a pipelike arrangement with larger openings which are resin ducts. In the fiber walls are tiny valves. *Courtesy: U.S. Forest Service Forest Products Laboratory*

Fig. 1.2 A cross section of a 62-year-old loblolly pine tree. It has been through a fire, drought, plague, and plenty: all this is recorded in its rings. Each spring and summer the tree added new layers of wood to its trunk. Wood formed in spring grows faster and is lighter because it consists of large cells. In summer, growth is slower; the wood has smaller cells and is darker. By counting the dark rings, you can learn the tree's age and much more. Can you find out when the tree was touched by fire and when there were bad years? *Courtesy: St. Regis Paper Co.*

cross section of a tree, its rings can tell us a story of a tree's life: its age, difficult years, attacks by insects, storms that caused loss of limbs, and so on. That is why each tree is unique.

Classification of Woods There are over 100,000 different varieties of trees from several hundred species (Fig. 1.3).

Some of the same woods can be found through much of the world where climatic conditions are similar.

There are two main classifications of wood: *softwood* and *hardwood* (*see* Fig. 1.1). Softwood comes from trees that have needlelike leaves. There are the pines, firs, holly, hemlock, and all the evergreens. They are classified as soft-

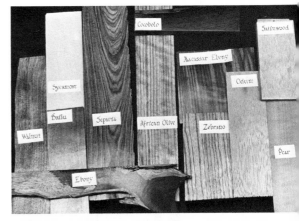

Fig. 1.3a and b Some examples of wood from all parts of the world. *Courtesy: Edwin Spencer*

wood mainly because they are non-porous but have large, open grains. They also tend to deteriorate faster than hardwood and, except for pine, soft-woods tend to split and sliver. Hardwoods include broad-leaved trees such as oak, cherry, walnut, ebony, mahogany, and so on. These are close-grained woods with small pores which tend to last for centuries.

One might assume, then, that soft-woods are softer than hardwoods. This is not so. Douglas fir and yews are soft-woods that are harder than poplar, aspen, and Philippine mahogany, which are hardwoods.

There are few generalizations that can be made about wood. And there are no absolutes, either, about working with wood. There are, however, some basic facts and approaches that do hold up for

the most part. Hardwoods, for instance, are usually more difficult to work than softwoods, but they lend themselves to more precise workmanship. Softwoods are more easily joined by nailing, whereas hardwoods require special fastening techniques because nails can either split the wood or double over.

There are certain consistencies in wood, even if their botanical names will differ within a species. For example, there are many different kinds of red oak. Their leaves, bark, and fruit may differ, but the wood is identical within the grouping, both in structure and appearance. When one looks at a piece of wood, then, identification as to which kind of red oak it is can be difficult.

There are also great differences among woods. Some woods are stronger and more attractive; some shrink less,

Fig. 1.4 Seasoning of wood in a shed outside John Makepeace's woodworking shop, England. Ends of wood are marked with different colors to indicate when the lumber was stacked.

resist decay, bend more easily; others can be cut and joined more precisely; some have predominant grains and variations in color. Woods are also non-uniform. Natural defects such as checks, which are cracks caused by stresses and improper seasoning, knots caused by branches, insect holes, fungi and rot, can change the appearance of woods within the same species. Also, the pattern of wood from the same species can differ because quicker growing years and slower growing years will affect the configurations. The way a tree grows during different seasons, the part of the tree from which wood is cut, and the manner in which wood is sawed will affect appearance too. Even wood from different parts of a tree will differ in cut, how easily it will cut, whether there are burls, or knots, and so on.

Seasoning and Drying Wood is designed to carry sap and water, and as long as a tree is alive its cells contain water. The day a tree is felled, it begins to dry and the wood loses its water with air moving in to fill the emptying spaces in the cells. As wood dries, it becomes lighter, harder, stronger, and smaller through shrinkage. Wood, though, never completely loses all of its water. Unless wood has just been dried in an oven, it holds a quantity of water—perhaps 12 percent of its own oven-dry weight. In a damp place or outdoors it holds more.

Shrinkage and attendant problems of warpage are some of the characteristics difficult to eliminate completely. There are ways, however, of minimizing the undesirable aspects of shrinkage and warpage. Much of this depends upon how wood is seasoned, or dried, and how it is cut.

The best way to season wood is to stack it outdoors, or in an open-sided shed so air can flow freely around any plank or piece (Fig. 1.4). The amount of time necessary for this first seasoning step varies with each type of wood and its thickness. Oak or ash can take over a year to season, others may take just a few months. Kiln seasoning is another method of drying wood. This happens slowly through artificial heat with a process that takes about ten days. After seasoning, it is a good idea to stack wood indoors for a few months before using it.

Carvers in countries such as Indonesia, the Ivory Coast, and Tanzania carve directly into raw or green wood because unseasoned wood is easier to carve. The resulting sculptures often crack or check later as the wood dries unevenly. If surfaces are sealed so that water escapes from the wood cells more slowly, then there is a possibility that cracking would be reduced.

LUMBER

Cutting Methods Probably the least expensive way to cut lumber, because it yields less waste and takes less labor to perform, is illustrated in Figure 1.5. The method is called *plain sawed* when it is hardwood, or *flat grained* when softwood. In this approach, wood is sawed at a tangent to the annual rings.

A more expensive method of cutting up a log is called *quarter sawing* if hardwood, and *edge grained* or *vertical grained* if softwood. First the wood is cut into quarters, then quarters are cut into boards. In this kind of cutting, lumber shrinks and swells less in width and warps less than in plain-sawed lumber.

Veneers are made by peeling or slicing wood that has been softened by hot water or steam. The thickness of veneer varies depending upon its final application, such as whether it is to be used for veneering furniture or to construct plywood. Veneers for furniture use generally range from $1/28''$ to $1/36''$ in thickness. Because they are so thin, veneers require gluing to a base, which is usually a cheaper grade of lumber.

Plywood is made by gluing separate veneers together with grains running at right angles to one another. The thickness of plywoods is usually described by the number of laminated veneers, e.g., 3, 5, or 9 ply or thickness.

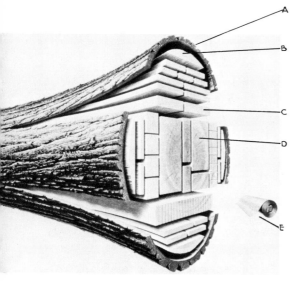

Fig. 1.5 How the tree is used
A. **Debarking the log** is essential to its full utilization because bark cannot be used for papermaking, and therefore any piece dropped in the chipper has to be free of bark. But the bark can be used for fuel and soil mulch.
B. **The rounded sides** of the log, called "slabs," are the first pieces sent to the chipper as the log goes through the sawmill. This idealized picture shows the entire log being used for lumber, except for the slabs. Actually, as cutting continues, other pieces go to the chipper, including edgings, trim ends, and other parts of the log not usable as lumber. Each log presents different problems and can be handled differently.
C. **The outer portions** of the log have the fewest knots. This "clear" lumber is usually made into boards or planks varying in thickness from 1–3 inches.
D. **Toward the center** of the log, knots increase and the wood is less suitable for boards. Heavier planks and square or rectangular beams are normally sawed from this section. The center of the log is used primarily for structural beams strong enough so that they are not weakened by knots. Knots are most frequent here because this is the oldest section of the tree. Branches that were removed during the early years of the tree's life left knots that were covered over as the tree grew outward.
E. **Plywood** is, in effect, a sandwich of thin wooden veneers. Veneer is made by "peeling," that is, holding a long blade against a rotating log. The wood is continuously peeled off, down to an 8-inch core. The core is then treated as though it were a small log. It can be made into lumber and, of course, the rounded portions go to the chipper.
Courtesy: St. Regis Paper Co.

Plywoods are strong in all directions and tend not to warp.

Laminboard and *blockboard* consist of blocks of wood glued as the interior of a sandwich between two outer veneers. This construction has many of the same advantages as plywood, except that the boards tend to be thicker than plywood.

Grading Woods Grading of solid lumber varies from place to place. Generally, softwood is graded by preparation and use, such as whether it is dry lumber—dried to a moisture content of 19% or less—or whether it is green lumber—containing an excess of 19% moisture—and whether it is considered *yard lumber* with pieces intended for construction of buildings; *structural lumber* where thickness is over two inches; or *factory and shop* lumber. For most purposes, the kind of lumber one would use for working with wood in art and craft would be this latter type.

There are grades within this softwood category as well. *Select wood,* the top category, has several grades: *A* is top quality, blemish free; *B* is blemish free; *C* has small defects, such as knots, and variable coloring; *D* has even more imperfections. In factory and shop lumber, there is still another category and that is *common* grades of boards. These are suitable for general construction purposes. Grading here ranges from number 1, which has small defects, all the way to number 4, which is rough, coarse, knotty wood, usually used for crating.

Hardwood grading is still different and is a very complicated process. To derive the most relevant aspect from the system, most commonly purchased grades of hardwood are rated FAS, meaning *firsts and seconds.* Most FAS lumber will have a minimum width of 6 inches and must be 8 feet or more in length, except for walnut and butternut, which are at least 5 inches wide and are selected for their color if they are quartersawed. FAS woods are graded from the poorer side of the board, so the other side may have fewer imperfections. *Selects* is the third grade, and still pretty good for most projects requiring only one good face. The least expensive grade consists of the *commons*. These are rated as Common #1, Common #2, sound, wormy, etc.; they are usually unsuitable for crafting purposes.

Purchasing Lumber The standard unit of measurement for solid lumber is the *board foot*. The board foot equals its thickness (measured in inches), times its width (measured in inches), times its length (also measured in inches). This amount is then divided by 144, yielding the board foot. Lumber is priced by the board foot. Sometimes, though, wood is also sold by the lineal foot; in other cases, it is sold by the pound.

The lumber dealer indicates the dimensions of a particular piece of wood for its thickness and width before drying or finishing. Therefore, the actual size you will be getting will be somewhat less than indicated on the bill. When measuring the amount of lumber you need for a particular project, it is best to figure one-third extra for waste. It might be useful for you to note that, when ordering wood, the following outline of a typical specification will help to ensure that you will get what you want.

Kind of wood: grain, color, figure, toughness (how hard it is to cut, nail into, etc.)
Number of pieces
Size: thickness, width, length
Grade: e.g., FAS or Common #1, etc.
Seasoning: kiln dried (KD) or air dried (AD)
Type of millwork: whether S2S (surfaced on two sides) or S1S (surfaced on one side)

The tables at the end of this chapter under Common Woods: Sources, Uses, and Characteristics will serve as guidelines to you in determining these specifications. For example, if your project will require a highly figured wood, Table H will help you to determine the type you want; if shrinkage or swelling of wood will be a primary factor in your project—a cabinet with doors that will be opened and closed frequently, for instance—Table F will help you to eliminate unsuitable woods and select the best for your purposes.

WOOD AS A THREE-DIMENSIONAL MATERIAL

Rather briefly, we have looked at wood as it grows and is processed for use. In the final analysis, what is truly important is to know how to work with wood, to know what it will do and what tools should be used to create a three-dimensional object. (Only veneers when employed in marquetry for picture making, can be considered two dimensional.) Wood, by virtue of its nature as a

Fig. 1.6 An old wooden beehive from Romania.

material that has height, width, and depth, is three dimensional. Working with wood, then, involves seeing forms on all sides, from all angles—quite different from looking at a painting or print only from the front.

Also, to be able to construct an object we must know—conceptually—how we can shape and form the material to realize its possibilities. Basically, we can utilize wood by cutting it, attaching it with joints, glue, or fasteners, bending it, turning it, carving it, and finishing it in various ways. Except for two dimensional applications, virtually every project would involve some aspects of the above. Then, when we utilize any of these concepts, we are, in effect, involved in a transformation process, significantly changing the shape of wood, yet allowing wood to be what it is: wood. We must never violate the integrity of

Fig. 1.7 A laminated hand-carved plywood platter by
Tapio Wirkkala, 10½ inches long. *Courtesy: Collection,
The Museum of Modern Art Gift of Georg Jensen, Inc.*

Fig. 1.8 A chess set with turned chess pieces of pine
and mahogany. The king is 16 inches high, pawns are 5
inches high, and the board is 3 feet square. *Copyright
and courtesy: Robin and Mary Ellis*

what lumber would be by forcing it into an imitative role, where wood looks like it could be something else.

COMMON WOODS: SOURCES, USES, AND CHARACTERISTICS

The following list will enable you to familiarize yourself with the attributes of frequently used woods and will make it easier to select the most appropriate type for a particular project. The data is derived from information supplied by the Forest Products Laboratory, Forest Service, U.S. Department of Agriculture.

ASH
Sources States east of the Rockies
Uses Benches, hammer handles, cabinets, ball bats, wagon construction
Characteristics Strong, heavy, hard, tough, elastic; close straight grain, shrinks very little, takes excellent finish, lasts long

BALSA
Source Ecuador
Uses Rafts, food boxes, lining of refrigerators, life preservers, loudspeakers, soundproofing, model airplane construction
Characteristics Lightest of all woods, very soft, strong for its weight, good heat-insulating qualities, odorless

BASSWOOD
Source Eastern half of the U.S., with the exception of coastal regions
Uses Low-grade furniture, cheaply constructed buildings, interior finish, shelving, drawers, boxes, drainboards, woodenware, novelties, general millwork
Characteristics Soft, very light, weak, brittle, not durable, shrinks considerably; inferior to poplar, but very uniform, works easily, takes screws and nails well, does not twist or warp

BEECH
Sources East of the Mississippi; southeastern Canada
Uses Cabinetwork, imitation mahogany furniture, wood dowels, boat trim, interior finish, tool handles, turnery, carving, flooring
Characteristics Similar to birch, but not so durable when exposed to weather, shrinks and checks considerably; close grain, light or dark red color

BIRCH
Sources East of Mississippi River and north of Gulf Coast states; southeastern Canada; Newfoundland
Uses Cabinetwork, imitation mahogany furniture, wood dowels, boat trim, interior finish, tool handles, turnery, carving
Characteristics Hard, durable, fine grain, even texture, heavy, stiff, strong, tough, takes high polish, works easily; forms excellent base for white enamel finish, but not durable when exposed; heartwood is light to dark reddish brown in color

BUTTERNUT
Sources Southern Canada; Minnesota; eastern U.S. as far south as Alabama and Florida
Uses Toys, altars, woodenware, mill-

work, interior trim, furniture, boats, scientific instruments

Characteristics Very much like walnut in color, but softer, not so soft as white pine and basswood; easy to work, coarse grained, fairly strong

CYPRESS

Sources Maryland to Texas; along Mississippi Valley to Illinois

Uses Small boat planking, siding, shingles, sash, doors, tanks, silos, railway ties

Characteristics Many characteristics similar to white cedar; water-resistant qualities make it excellent for use as boat planking

BLACK CHERRY

Sources Throughout Maine westward to eastern North Dakota and southward to central areas of Florida and Texas

Uses Furniture and cabinetry, plates and other woodenware

Characteristics Hard, stiff and strong; resistant to shock; moderately large shrinkage; comparatively free from checking and warping; difficult to work with handtools; ranks high in bending strength

DOUGLAS FIR

Sources Pacific Coast; British Columbia

Uses Deck planking on large ships, filling pieces and bulkheads of small boats, building construction, plywood

Characteristics Excellent structural lumber, strong, easy to work, clear straight grain, soft but brittle; heartwood is durable in contact with ground, best structural timber of northwest

ELM

Sources States east of Colorado

Uses Wheel-stock, boats, furniture

Characteristics Slippery, heavy, hard, tough, durable; difficult to split, not resistant to decay

HICKORY

Sources Arkansas, Ohio, Kentucky, Tennessee

Uses Tools, handles, wagon stock, hoops, baskets, wagon spokes

Characteristics Very heavy, hard, stronger and tougher than other native woods, but checks, shrinks; difficult to work, subject to decay and insect attack

LIGNUM VITAE

Source Central America

Uses Water-exposed shaft bearings of small boats and ships; tool handles, small turned articles, mallet heads

Characteristics Dark greenish brown, unusually hard, close grained, very heavy, resinous; difficult to split and work, has soapy feeling

LIVE OAK

Sources Southern Atlantic and Gulf coasts of U.S.; Oregon and California

Uses Implements, wagons, ship building

Characteristics Very heavy, hard, tough, strong, durable, difficult to work; light brown or yellow, sapwood nearly white

MAHOGANY

Sources Honduras, Mexico, Central America, Florida, West Indies, central Africa, other tropical sections

Uses Fine furniture, boats, decks, fixtures, interior trim in expensive homes, musical instruments

Characteristics Brown to red color, one of most useful of cabinet woods, hard, durable, does not split easily; open grained, takes beautiful finish when grain is filled, but checks, swells, shrinks, warps slightly

MAPLE

Sources All states east of Colorado; southern Canada

Uses Excellent furniture, high-grade floors, tool handles, countertops, bowling pins

Characteristics Fine grained, grain often curly or "birds' eyes"; heavy, tough, hard, strong, rather easy to work, but not durable; heartwood is light brown, sapwood is nearly white

NORWAY PINE

Sources States bordering Great Lakes

Use Interior trim

Characteristics Light, fairly hard, strong, not durable in contact with ground

PHILIPPINE MAHOGANY

Source Philippine Islands

Uses Pleasure boats, medium-grade furniture, interior trim

Characteristics Not a true mahogany; shrinks, expands, splits, warps, but available in long, wide clear boards

POPLAR

Sources Virginias, Kentucky, Tennessee, Mississippi Valley

Uses Low-grade furniture, cheaply constructed buildings, interior finish, shelving, drawers, boxes

Characteristics Soft, cheap, obtainable in wide boards; warps, shrinks, rots easily; light, brittle, weak, but works easily and holds nails well; fine texture

RED CEDAR

Sources East of Colorado and north of Florida

Uses Mothproof chests, lining for linen closets, sills, other uses similar to those for white cedar

Characteristics Very light, soft, weak, brittle; low shrinkage, great durability, fragrant scent, generally knotty; beautiful when finished in natural color, easily worked

RED OAK

Sources Virginias, Ohio, Tennessee, Kentucky, Arkansas, Missouri, Maryland

Uses Interior finish, furniture, cabinets, millwork, crossties when preserved

Characteristics Tends to warp, coarse grain, does not last well when exposed to weather; porous, easily impregnated with preservative; heavy, tough, strong

REDWOOD

Source California

Uses General construction, paneling

Characteristics Inferior to yellow pine and fir in strength, shrinks and splits little; extremely soft, light, straight grained, very durable and exceptionally decay resistant

SPRUCE

Sources New York, New England, West Virginia; central Canada; Great Lakes States; Idaho, Oregon, Washington

Uses Resonance wood, airplanes, oars, masts, spars, baskets

Characteristics Light, soft, low strength, fair durability, close grain, yellowish, sapwood indistinct

SUGAR PINE
Sources California, Oregon
Uses Same as for white pine
Characteristics Very light, soft; resembles white pine

TEAK
Sources India, Burma, Java, Thailand
Uses Deck planking, shaft logs for small boats
Characteristics Light brown color, strong, easily worked, durable, resistant to damage from moisture

WALNUT
Sources Eastern half of U.S., except southern Atlantic and Gulf coasts; some in New Mexico, Arizona, California
Uses Expensive furniture, cabinets, interior woodwork; gun stocks, tool handles, airplane propellers, fine boats, musical instruments
Characteristics Fine cabinet wood, coarse grain but takes beautiful finish; medium weight, hard, strong, easily worked, brittle, dark chocolate color, does not warp or check

WHITE CEDAR
Sources Eastern coast of U.S.; around Great Lakes
Uses Boat planking, shingles, siding, poles
Characteristics Soft, lightweight, close grained, exceptionally durable when exposed to water; not strong enough for building construction, brittle, low shrinkage, fragments, generally knotty

WHITE OAK
Sources Virginias, Ohio, Tennessee, Kentucky, Missouri, Maryland, Indiana, Arkansas
Uses Boat and ship stems, sternposts, fenders, transoms, framing for buildings, hard-wearing furniture, tool handles, agricultural implements, fence posts
Characteristics Heavy, hard, strong, medium-coarse grain, tough, dense; most durable of hardwoods, elastic, rather easy to work, but shrinks and is likely to check; light brownish gray in color with reddish tinge, medullary rays are large and outstanding and present beautiful figures when quarter sawed; receives high polish

WHITE PINE
Sources Minnesota, Maine, Wisconsin, Idaho, Michigan, Montana, Washington, Oregon, California
Uses Patterns, any interior or exterior job that doesn't require maximum strength; window sash, interior trim, millwork, cabinets, cornices
Characteristics Easy to work, fine straight grain, free of knots, takes excellent finish; durable when exposed to water, expands when wet, shrinks when dry; soft, white, nails without splitting, not very strong

YELLOW PINE
Source Virginia to Texas
Uses Most important lumber for heavy construction and exterior work; risings, filling pieces, clamps, floors, bulkheads of small boats, posts, piling, paving blocks

Characteristics Hard, strong, heartwood is durable in the ground; grain varies, heavy, tough, reddish brown in color, resinous, medullary rays well marked

The following section of tables classifies common woods according to desirable and not-so-desirable traits. Again, these will be of use to you in determining the most suitable wood to use for a specific purpose.

Table A. Comparative Ease of Working with Hand Tools

EASIEST
Basswood
Cedar
   northern white
   southern white
   western red
Pine
   northern white
   ponderosa
   sugar
   western white
Poplar, yellow

INTERMEDIATE
Cedar, eastern red
Chestnut
Cottonwood
Cypress, southern
Fir
   balsam

   white
Gum, red
Hemlock
   eastern
   western
Redwood
Spruce
   eastern
   Engelmann
   Sitka
Walnut

HARDEST
Ash
   black
   white
Beech
Birch, yellow
Cherry
Douglas fir

Elm
   rock
   soft
Hackberry
Hickory
   pecan
   true
Larch, western
Locust
   black
   honey
Maple
   hard
   soft
Oak
   red
   white
Pine, southern yellow
Sycamore
Tupelo

Table B. Comparative Ease of Planing Hardwoods

LEAST DIFFICULT	Poplar, yellow	MOST DIFFICULT
Beech		Birch, sweet
Gum	INTERMEDIATE	Cottonwood
red	Ash	Elm, soft
sap	Basswood	Hickory
Hackberry	Buckeye	Maple
Magnolia	Chestnut	hard
Oak	Gum	soft
chestnut	black	Sycamore
red	tupelo	Willow
white	Pecan	

Table C. Comparative Toughness

LEAST TOUGH	Chestnut	TOUGHEST
Basswood	Cottonwood	Ash
Cedar	Cypress, southern	black
northern white	Douglas fir	white
southern white	Gum, red	Beech
western red	Hemlock	Birch, yellow
Fir	eastern	Elm
balsam	western	rock
white	Larch, western	soft
Maple, soft	Pine	Hackberry
Pine	southern yellow	Hickory
northern white	western white	pecan
ponderosa	Redwood	true
sugar	Spruce	Locust
Poplar, yellow	eastern	black
Spruce, Engelmann	Sitka	honey
	Sycamore	Maple
MODERATELY TOUGH	Tupelo	Oak
Cedar, eastern red		red
Cherry		white
		Walnut

Table D. Relative Hardness

SOFTEST	INTERMEDIATE	
Basswood	Chestnut	Elm
Butternut	Cypress	rock
Cedar	southern	soft
northern white	Douglas fir	Hackberry
southern white	Gum, red	Hickory
western red	Hemlock	pecan
Cottonwood	eastern	true
Fir	western	Larch, western
balsam	Redwood	Locust
white		black
Pine		honey
northern white		Maple
ponderosa	HARDEST	hard
sugar	Ash	soft
western white	black	Oak
Poplar, yellow	white	red
Spruce	Beech	white
eastern	Birch, yellow	Pine, southern yellow
Engelmann	Cedar	Sycamore
Sitka	eastern red	Tupelo
	Cherry	Walnut

From Donald G. Coleman, "Properties, Selection, and Suitability of Woods for Woodworking," Forest Products Laboratory, Forest Service, U.S. Department of Agriculture

Table E. Comparative Freedom from Warping

LEAST WARP	INTERMEDIATE	
Cedar	Ash	Locust
eastern red	white	black
northern white	black	honey
southern white	Basswood	Maple
western red	Birch, yellow	hard
Cherry	Cypress, southern	soft
Chestnut	Douglas fir	Oak
Pine	Elm, rock	red
northern white	Fir	white
ponderosa	balsam	Pine
sugar	white	southern yellow
western white	Hackberry	
Poplar, yellow	Hemlock	
Redwood	eastern	MOST WARP
Spruce	western	Beech
eastern	Hickory	Cottonwood
Engelmann	pecan	Elm, soft
Sitka	true	Gum, red
Walnut	Larch, western	Sycamore
		Tupelo

From Donald G. Coleman, "Properties, Selection, and Suitability of Woods for Woodworking," Forest Products Laboratory, Forest Service, U.S. Department of Agriculture

Table F. Tendency of Woods to Shrink and Swell

MINIMUM	MODERATE	
Ash, black	Ash, white	southern yellow
Basswood	Cherry	western white
Beech	Chestnut	Poplar, yellow
Birch, yellow	Cypress, southern	Spruce
Cottonwood	Fir	eastern
Elm	balsam	Engelmann
rock	Douglas	Sitka
soft	white	Tupelo
Gum, red	Hemlock	Walnut
Hackberry	eastern	MAXIMUM
Hickory	western	Cedar
pecan	Larch, western	eastern red
true	Locust	northern white
Maple, hard	black	southern white
Oak	honey	western red
red	Maple, soft	Pine
white	Pine	northern white
Sycamore	ponderosa	sugar
		Redwood

From Donald G. Coleman, "Properties, Selection, and Suitability of Woods for Woodworking," Forest Products Laboratory, Forest Service, U.S. Department of Agriculture

Table G. Retention of Odor and Taste When Dry

LOW	soft	honey
Ash, white	Poplar, yellow	
Basswood	Spruce	
Beech	eastern	HIGH
Birch, yellow	Engelmann	Cedar
Elm	Sitka	eastern red
rock	Tupelo	northern white
soft		southern white
Fir		western red
balsam	INTERMEDIATE	Douglas fir
white	Cherry	Larch, western
Hackberry	Chestnut	Pine
Hemlock	Cottonwood	northern white
eastern	Cypress, southern	ponderosa
western	Gum, red	southern yellow
Maple	Locust	sugar
hard	black	western white

From Donald G. Coleman, "Properties, Selection, and Suitability of Woods for Woodworking," Forest Products Laboratory, Forest Service, U.S. Department of Agriculture

Table H. Comparative Amount of Figure in Woods

HIGHLY FIGURED	MODULATED FIGURE	
Ash	Beech	Redwood
black	Birch, yellow	Spruce
white	Cedar, red	eastern
Chestnut	eastern, western	Engelmann
Cypress, southern	Cherry	Sitka
Douglas fir	Fir	Sycamore
Elm	balsam	Walnut
rock	white	
soft	Gum, red	LEAST FIGURE
Hackberry	Hemlock	Basswood
Larch, western	eastern	Cedar
Locust	western	northern white
black	Hickory	southern white
honey	pecan	Cottonwood
Oak	true	Pine
red	Maple	northern white
white	hard	ponderosa
Pine	soft	sugar
southern yellow	Poplar, yellow	western white
		Tupelo

From Donald G. Coleman, "Properties, Selection, and Suitability of Woods for Woodworking," Forest Products Laboratory, Forest Service, U.S. Department of Agriculture
Note: Woods classed in the table as highly figured will have a pronounced figure in an ordinary commercial run. Those with a more modulated figure sometimes require special selection to obtain the desired figure. Woods classed as low are seldom satisfactory when figure is desired.

TOOLS AND EQUIPMENT

In order to be in control and command the evolvement of the wooden form that we originally conceive, we have to know what tools will do to wood and then how to process wood with these tools.

Wood has been around a long time and all kinds of tools and machinery have been invented to cope with design problems. Highly complex woodworking shops have emerged, but the products coming out of these shops are not necessarily more successful than ob-

jects that are created with the most basic equipment and tools.

There appear to be three levels of equipment. At the first level there are basic hand tools such as a hammer, knife, coping, tenon, and crosscut saws, screwdriver, hand drill, plane, chisels, mallet, clamps and/or vise, awl, pliers, and ruler—few other tools are necessary. But at the next level, it is nice to have hand power tools, such as a drill with its assortment of attachments from drill and router bits to sanding disks, a hand-held sabre saw, orbital sander, hand-held circular saw, and a few other tools on this level, such as a miter box. None of these tools takes up too much space, nor do they require a heavy investment in money. On the third level, however, the cost of motor-driven equipment can only be justified if the amount of work turned out warrants it, or if you can afford to invest in it. Here we have a variety of planers, drill presses, routers, lathes, radial-arm saws, band saws, table saws, belt and disk sanders, and so on. Costs vary greatly from the so-called hobby equipment to industrial-type machines. Woodworking benches, steam-bending equipment, assorted chisels, bits of various types, gougers, scrapers, spoke shavers, measuring implements, punches, Surform tools, and so on, do accumulate as we begin to produce and as specific projects warrant it. Very few woodworkers, surrounded by the temptations of all the machines and gadgetry available, can resist and hold tools and equipment down to a minimum level!

CUTTING INSTRUMENTS

We can start with a basic piece of lumber, cut it into shapes and then work out means of attaching the shapes (In forming joints for attaching parts—except when fasteners such as screws or only glue is employed—some kind of cutting is necessary here as well). Or we can begin with a thick chunk of wood

and carve away unwanted areas. The result is called *monolyxous* because the end product was fashioned from a single whole piece of wood and no parts were attached. Bowls and sculptures are frequently formed this way.

Most woodworking tools cut away, drill into, remove surfaces, gouge, or carve into wood. Even materials, machines, and tools used for finishing refine and finish the surface in some way and, in doing so, remove some of the wood's surface. The question that is vital to ask is, What will cut the lumber best for a particular operation?

Woodworking Handsaws If one is to cut along the grain or across the grain of a piece of wood in a basic cutting operation, different kinds of saws are necessary. The design of the teeth of the *crosscut saw* for cutting across the grain are sharpened on alternate sides and bent or "set" slightly outwards (Fig. 2.1). This makes for blade clearance and enables the saw to cut through freely; otherwise the blade would bind.

The *rip saw* is a saw that cuts with the grain. The teeth of this saw are filed at right angles to the sides and the cutting action is on the downward thrust when each tooth acts as a small chisel, cutting off a minute part of the wood fiber ends, thereby working its way through the wood.

The *back saw* is a fine tooth, crosscut saw with a heavy metal band across the top to help strengthen its thin blade (Fig. 2.1). It is used to make fine cuts for joinery and is also used in a *miter box.*

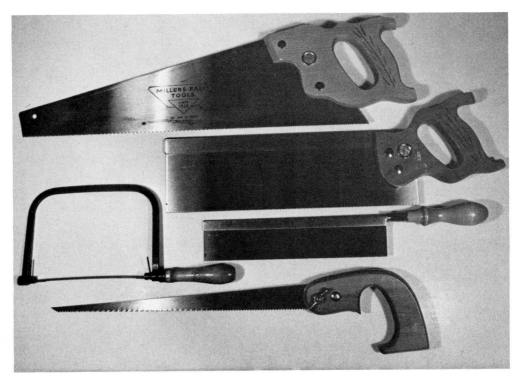

Fig. 2.1 Hand-held saws (from *top*): crosscut saw, back
saw, dovetail saw, coping saw, compass saw.

As shown in Figure 2.2, the miter box is
a device for guiding a handsaw at the
proper angle to bevel individual pieces
for fitting together in a miter joint.

The *tenon saw* is a saw with a thin
blade that is supported and held in tension by a brass or steel collar along the
top or back edge. Tenon saws can be
used for cutting small pieces of wood,
either with or across the grain. The
dovetail saw is similar to a tenon saw,
but is shorter and often has the same
kind of a handle as found on a chisel
(*see* Fig. 2.1). It is used for cutting small

sections out of wood for making joints.

The rip and crosscut saws are used
for cutting rough dimensions from a
board. Usually the board is supported
by hand over the edge of a flat cutting
surface, while the saw is manipulated in
a back-and-forth movement by the other
hand. Dovetail and tenon saws are used
only when the wood is fixed in a vise.

The *compass saw* is a saw containing
a tapered blade from 12–14 inches long
and used to cut gentle curves or inside
curves (Fig. 2.1).

Similar to the compass saw is the *key-*

Fig. 2.2 Miter box and back saw.

hole saw which has a narrower taper, finer teeth, and is about 10–12 inches long. The keyhole saw is used to cut small openings and finer curves.

Another saw employed for cutting curves, holes, and scroll work, as well as shaping the ends of moldings for joints, is the *coping saw* (Fig. 2.1). This is a U-shaped saw frame that contains in tension along the bottom a very narrow and fine blade. As curves are cut, the blade can be turned to adjust for the angle of the cut.

Hand-Held Machine Saws The *portable circular saw* is available in various sizes and contains a circular blade. Different kinds of blades can be used, depending upon the most frequent operations. A combination blade for both

crosscutting and ripping is most commonly employed. A great advantage to using this portable tool is that the saw can be operated on location. In most operations some kind of *fence* (a strip of metal or wood anchored into place) is necessary to guide the hand-held saw toward straight cuts. The angle of the blade can be adjusted to *bevel* (cut or slope an edge to an oblique angle) a cut, but only straight cuts are satisfactory with this type of saw.

The *bayonet* or *saber saw* is smaller and useful for cutting all types of curves because the blade is narrower (Fig. 2.3). It is relatively easy to control. Its blade, which resembles a saber, can also cut holes. Several types of blades are available for the saber saw as well. Perhaps the most useful are a fast scroll-cutting

Fig. 2.3 Saber saw used to cut all types of curves.

blade with six teeth per inch, about 4½ inches long—good for roughing-in work—and the finer fast scroll-cutting blade with ten teeth per inch, about 3⅝ inches long. When inside cuts are made, one must start with a drilled hole large enough to insert the blade, then the cutting action can begin. For ripping or straight cuts, a guide or fence should be clamped into place first.

Stationary Machine Saws The *circular table saw* is a basic piece of equipment for a well-equipped shop. It consists of a heavy table that contains the motor. The saw blade, which is adjusted with a handwheel, sticks up through the table in varying heights (usually from 3–7 inches) and angles, depending upon the size of the equipment. The kinds of blades vary according to use, as well; a combination blade is the most versatile. A fence is part of the table saw and is used for guiding the straight cuts that are made on it. *This machine can also be a dangerous piece of equipment. At no time should a piece of wood be fed toward the blade by using your hand.* Only a notched piece of wood should be employed to steer the wood through the cutting operation. Never clear scraps away with your fingers. For clean cuts, the blade should clear the top of the wood by about ⅛–¼ inch.

The *radial-arm* or *radial saw* is another versatile and important piece of equipment. If you can only afford one straight-cutting table-mounted saw,

then the radial-arm saw will perform most straight cutting operations. In addition, it can function as a shaper, jointer, drill, boring tool, sander, router, and wood lathe—depending upon the angle of the saw motor and the attachments used. The saw blade and motor are suspended on an arm (which can swing) above the table, and depending upon the width of the piece, the blade is pulled across the work toward you. In some operations, where the work is very long, the saw blade is turned, reversed, and the wood is fed into the blade. *Care must be taken here never to place fingers in the way of the blade, or to feed work without the use of a pushing tool.* Blades come in various types and diameters. Cuts can be mitered and beveled because the arm can swing in a radius of 180° and can be set at an angle.

The *band saw* is designed for cutting curved or irregular shapes, although it also can be used for straight cutting. The blade of the band saw is narrow (from ⅛–1½ inches) and its ends are welded together so that it forms a circular shape. Part of the blade goes around a wheel mounted above the table area, and the other part rides around a similar wheel that is attached below the table area. The saw travels through a slit in the table. Sizes of band saws vary enormously, from hobby types to heavy industrial ones. The size determines the thickness of the work that can be cut. It is limited to the distance between the table top and the blade guide when it is set at its uppermost point. It is possible to tilt the table of a band saw, and thereby the wood to be cut, allowing for bevels to be cut. The wood is fed into the blade away from the user, with the feed going as fast as the blade will take it; otherwise the blade will burn. If the blade will not take a certain radius of a curve at first cut, successive cuts may be necessary.

A *jig* or *scroll saw* is used for cutting curved or irregular work. It can be used for making inside cuts without cutting through the stock itself. Jigsaws vary in size from industrial equipment to small hobby models that are portable. It consists of a worktable containing a slit. A narrow, thin blade fits vertically through this slit and is attached to a mechanism above and below the table. The cutting action is, unlike the band saw's circular motion of traveling around a wheel, mainly an up-and-down slicing action. Some jigsaws are equipped with variable speed attachments, or operate at one or two adjusted speeds. The thickness of work, here too, depends upon the distance of the blade area from table to top arm. Unlike the band saw, the blade of the jigsaw can be easily removed and threaded through a drilled hole in the piece, allowing inside cuts to be made. Blades vary from rough cutting blades to finely toothed blades.

Surface-Cutting Tools This group of cutting tools scrapes, slices, routs, shaves, or chisels away smaller amounts of wood than the various saws we have discussed. These operations follow the preliminary or basic contouring or cutting of the wood.

Among the most frequently used surface-cutting implements are the hand-held planes. These vary from the *smooth plane* or *bench plane* shown in Figure 2.5, used for general surfacing and for small work, to a *jack plane*, which is ideal for smoothing rough, coarser surfaces. The jack plane is

Fig. 2.4 Dremel #550 Moto-Saw, a type of scroll saw. *Courtesy: Dremel Manufacturing Co.*

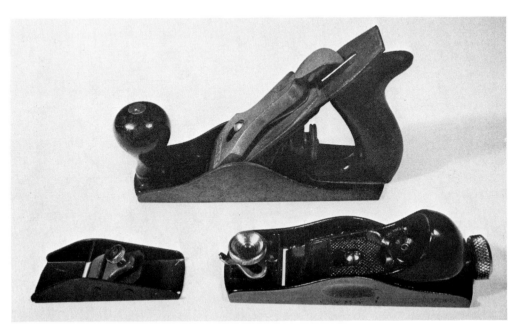

Fig. 2.5 Planes: (*top*) bench or smooth plane; (*left*) small trimming plane; (*right*) block plane.

about 7 inches longer (14–15 inches long) than a smooth plane. A *fore plane,* on the other hand, is even larger (18 inches long) and is used to shave a fine, flat finish on a long surface and along edges.

A *block plane* is a small plane with a single low-angle cutter, with the bevel up (Fig. 2.5). It is used to plane end grain or small pieces, and ends of trims and moldings. A *small trimming plane* (Fig. 2.5) fits into the palm of the hand and is used to refine small areas of small items.

The *spokeshave* is a small, planelike tool with a winglike handle on each side of a steel scraper. These shave away thin layers of wood. Steel scrapers are available also in various contours, as well as straight sides, to smooth a surface.

Gouges, carving tools, and *chisels* also cut away surfaces. The chisel has a bevel on one end and a flat side, whereas the gouge has various diameters of curved blades. Gouges cut away surfaces in irregular, curved slivers. Chisels trim, shape, and cut wood as for joints or edges (Fig. 2.6). Both have handles like that of a screwdriver, and both can be honed to razor-sharp cutting edges. *Carving tools* generally are smaller than gouges and chisels and perform similar but finer operations, mainly for surface and decorative effects (Fig. 2.6).

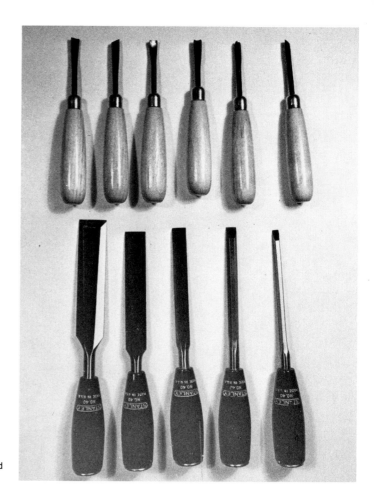

Fig. 2.6 Woodcarving tools (*top*) and a set of wood chisels.

Surform tools are available in plane file types and in curved blade types (Fig. 2.7). Their mountings may also vary from single to double handled types. Generally, the Surform has a blade containing multiple small cutting surfaces. These are used for cutting and trimming and are capable of producing smooth surfaces over curved areas.

And of course, among the hand-held cutting tools, there are *knives*. These come in a variety of shapes and blades and are utilized to cut, carve, trim wood and veneer. Several basic useful knives are shown in Figure 2.8.

A *jointer* is a motor-driven machine used for planing the surfaces and edges of wood that has been cut on a saw.

Knife blades, mounted into a cutter head, rotate as wood is fed over the blade. The height of the blades is adjusted by rotating a wheel set beneath the table. The smoothness of the cut depends upon the speed of rotation, the number of knives, and the unhesitating motion of the feed. A fence, similar to the one used on a circular saw, is used to guide the wood. The knives revolve at 3500–4500 rpm. Sizes of jointers vary from hobby equipment to heavy industrial types.

The *router* can be considered an edge-cutting tool. Routers vary from portable, motor-driven varieties to those set in tables. They are widely used for shaping the surfaces and edges of

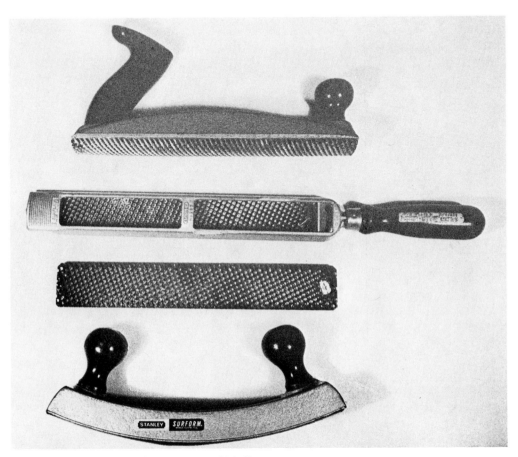

Fig. 2.7 Surform tools: (from *top*) plane type with half-round regular cut blade, file type, flat blade, and double-handle curved plane type.

wood and for forming joints. When using a portable router, the work is held stationary while the tool is moved along a path set by fences or jigs. When mounted in a table, the wood is fed along the edge of the rotating router blade. Routers operate at high speeds, 20,000 to 28,000 rpm. Various kinds of bits can be used in the router, depending upon the kind of work and shape desired.

DRILLING AND BORING TOOLS

In woodworking, the term *drilling* is used to denote holes ¼ inch in diameter or smaller, and *boring* refers to forming holes larger than ¼ inch in diameter. Drilling and boring tools are used to form holes of various dimensions in wood. They vary from hand-operated tools to many different varieties of machine-driven types.

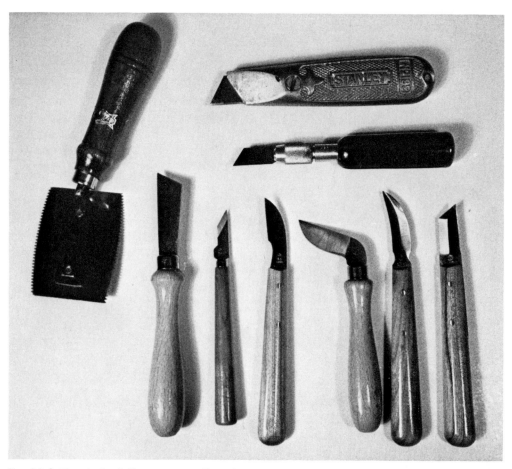

Fig. 2.8 Cutting tools: (*left*) veneer saw, (from *top center*) utility knife, X-acto knife, chip carving knives.

The auger bit, dowel bit, expansion bit, and Foerstner bits are used with a brace. Two common types of braces are the *plain brace* which operates in a full swinging circular motion, and a *ratchet type brace* which is used for cutting holes in close corners where the swinging motion of a brace would be restricted. The *auger bit,* which comes in a double or single-twist variety, has a screw shape at its point (Fig. 2.9). This type of bit is used to bore holes ¼ inch or larger. Of the two, the single twist bit is better for boring deep holes. The *dowel bit* is similar but has fewer twists; it is used primarily to drill holes for making dowel joints. The *expansion bit* shown in Figure 2.10 is one that holds cutters of various sizes which are attached to its base to bore holes larger

Fig. 2.9 Bits: (from *left*) spade type speed bore, spur center with machine thread, spur center double twist with ½-inch shank, twist drill, double twist auger bit with extension lip and spur, Foerstner bit, Greenly bit.

than one inch. The *Foerstner bit* (Fig. 2.9) will bore shallow holes and leave a flat bottom, unlike the expansion bit. But like the expansion bit, it will bore holes in thin stock and in end grain wood.

The *twist drill* (Fig. 2.9) comes in fractional-sized sets from $1/64$ inch to ½ inch and over, and is the most commonly used type. It fits into a hand drill. The *hand drill* shown in Figure 2.10,

fitted with a three-jaw chuck that is adjustable, will hold the twist drills for drilling small holes.

The more versatile of the motor-operated drills is the *portable hand drill* (Fig. 2.11). These vary in size and horsepower ratings. The most common sizes are those that take bit shanks up to ¼ inch or ½ inch in diameter. Most of these tools are equipped with a trigger

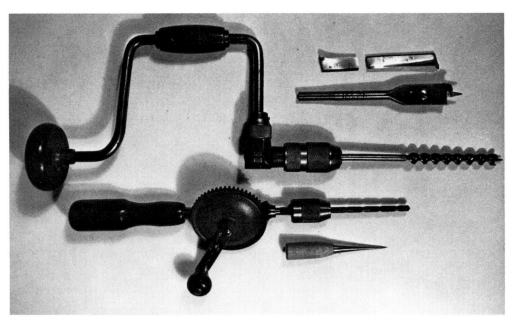

Fig. 2.10 (*Top right*) expansion bit with three interchangeable cutters, (*center*) self-centering chuck box ratchet, (second from *bottom*) hand drill with three-jaw chuck, (*bottom right*) awl.

switch that activates the twisting action.

Boring larger holes is best accomplished on stationary equipment such as *stationary drill presses*. There are bench type and floor type varieties that vary in size according to the capability of boring a certain diameter hole. For instance, a 10-inch drill press will bore a hole through the center of a piece of wood 10 inches in diameter. Most of these stationary drill presses are adjustable for variable speeds, depending upon how the speed pulley is attached in the pulley arrangement.

The range of bits for stationary equipment is even greater than for hand-held varieties. There are speed bits, plug cutters, and spur machine bits, among others. The *spur machine bit* (Fig. 2.9) has a brad and lip point and is a fast, clean-cutting bit for cutting dowel holes. The *speed bit,* sometimes called the *flat-power bit* or *spade bit* because it looks somewhat like a spade (Fig. 2.9), varies in sizes from ¼ inch to 1 inch, and is made with variable cutter heads.

In fine cabinet work, the heads of screws are recessed and then filled with a plug. To accomplish this, there are special *plug cutters* that vary in size; they cut out small plugs that can be inserted later in the hole, hiding the screw

Fig. 2.11 Single-speed electric hand drill with an assortment of accessories: flap sanding wheel; (*center left*) electrichisel and Allen wrench for dado, rabbit, and mortise cutting; (*center right*) shaper bit, standard drill bit, Surform drum; (*right*) sanding disk.

head and at the same time matching the wood and nearly rendering the attachment spot invisible.

SANDING MACHINES

The most basic sanding tool is *sand-paper,* powered by the hand. In many ways the hand is one of the most sensitive "machines" because the fingertips can vary pressure and locations of sanding. The bare fingertip also judges whether a job has been well done. Hand sanding has two small disadvantages—it takes more time and is tiring.

Sandpapers vary to accommodate all degrees and types of sanding. They come coated with various types of abrasives and in many degrees of grit size.

Most of the time the nomenclature is as follows: #200–400 grit numbers are considered *very fine* and are used to precede polishing, finishing before and after staining, and varnishing. *Fine* grits vary from #120–180 and are used for finish sanding just before staining or sealing. The *medium* grits have greater or faster cutting power, vary from #60–100 grit, and are used to remove rough textures. *Coarse* grits are from #50 down to #36 for sanding after the very rough texture is removed. And *very coarse* grits, #30 down to #16, are used only on very rough, unfinished surfaces.

Sanding machines vary from portable types such as the rotary belt and double-action sanders, to those attached to a hand drill, and various sized machines such as belt and drum disk

Fig. 2.12 Orbital and straight-action electric sander.

sanders. With the *belt sander,* the sanding is done as the sander is continually moved by hand and is never allowed to stand still for any length of time, else grooves will form. This is true of any hand-held sanding tool. The rotary action portable sanders are good for fast, rough sanding and for larger areas. The *orbital* or *straight-action sander* shown in Figure 2.12 (sometimes available in the same unit as a double-action sander) is best for finishing work and removal of finishes.

Of the stationary varieties, the belt sander can be adjusted to a horizontal table position or a vertical position. Often a *disk sanding unit* is attached to the same machine (Fig. 2.13). To perform surface sanding, the work is fed by hand across the belt by applying light, firm pressure and allowing the belt to do the work. The disk is best for end grain

Fig. 2.13 Professional disk sander.

sanding. Most disk sanding is done freehand. The drum sander is a drum shape equipped with a tubelike shape of sandpaper (Fig. 2.11). As it rotates, curved shapes can be finely formed or finished with this type of sander. Some hand-held sanding equipment can be made stationary with various attachments and then used as stationary machines.

LATHES AND WOOD-TURNING TOOLS

Wood lathes, at one point, were designed for the very experienced woodworker. There is another vocabulary and approach to turning wood than for woodcarving and construction. Recently available, however, is a low cost lathe, manufactured by Dremel Manufacturing Company, that permits the turning of small forms, no longer than about 6 inches (see Fig. 7.1). With the standard floor-type models, it is possible to form larger pieces and turn between centers (two points on the left and right of the lathe) and to turn a piece that has been temporarily attached to the end of the lathe. Detailed discussion of the lathe and its use in spindle and faceplate turning appears in Chapter 7.

Tools used are specially designed for turning and consist of *gouges* for roughing wood to a round shape; *diamond* or *spear-pointed* tools to finish insides, recesses, or corners; *parting tools* to recess parts or separate them;

skews to smooth and finish surfaces; *flat tools* for scraping recesses; and *round nose tools* for scraping concave recesses. While the wood is being turned, the tool, resting upon a tool rest, is used to cut away thin curls of wood.

MEASURING IMPLEMENTS

Among the most basic tools, and perhaps the most frequently used, are measuring implements. These vary from simple *rulers*—tape, straight, or folding—to more sophisticated ones, such as *marking gauges* and *calipers* or *dividers* of various types. Examples of several are shown in Figure 2.14. The pencil, to mark a spot or draw a line, and the awl (Fig. 2.10), to inscribe a spot or scratch a line, work hand-in-hand with rulers.

A *try square* or *right-angle gauge* is used for squaring and measuring, to test for angle and whether a surface is level. A *carpenter's level* is also used to judge: the levelness of a table top of a machine when adjusting tools, the floor when paralleling of surfaces is important, or a portable surface before it is fixed into place.

All measuring tools help indicate size, what size some part should be, and the matching of sizes on external or internal surfaces. Tools like calipers are used where rulers cannot fit. The distance between their two points is then translated to the straight edge of a ruler to judge for size or match.

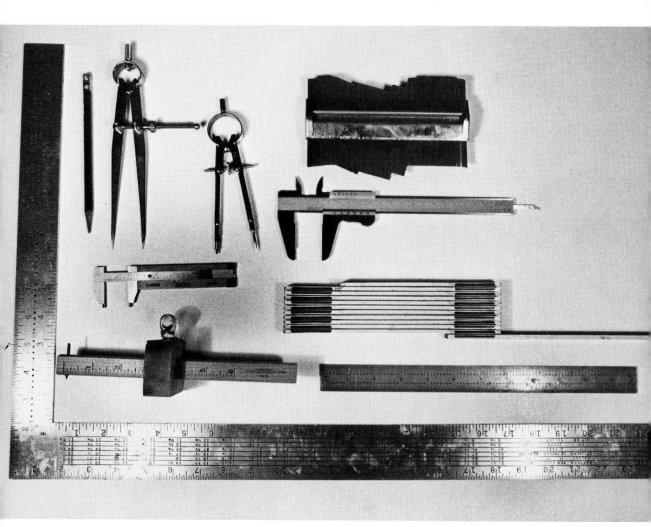

Fig. 2.14 Measuring devices: (*left*) steel flat square, (*top, left* to *right*) two dividers, contour measurer with Vernier caliper underneath; (*center, left* to *right*) inside measuring pocket caliper rule, folding extension rule; (*bottom, left* to *right*) hardwood marking gauges, metal ruler.

VISES AND CLAMPING TOOLS

Essential tools where there are gluing operations and the need for a third, steady hand, are *vises* and assorted types of *clamps* (called *cramps* in England). Vises are available in portable varieties that are held secure through suction, or those that screw to a tabletop for support, allowing their jaws to be used. Another type of vise is nonportable, permanently fixed, and usually attached to the woodworking bench.

Clamps are entirely portable and are used to hold pieces of work together for various operations, but mainly after applying glue. One of the best types for woodworking is *hand screw* or *wooden parallel clamps*. They come in a variety of sizes, from $5/0$ with a jaw length of 4 inches and a maximum opening between the jaws of 2 inches, to size 7 which is 24 inches long and has a maximum opening between the jaws of 17 inches. To operate this clamp, each hand holds a spindle handle while

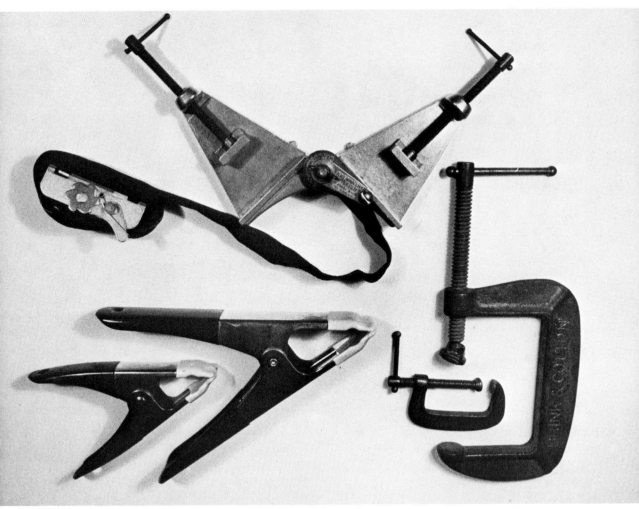

Fig. 2.15 Clamps: (*top left*) web clamp or band clamp, (*top*) corner clamp, (*bottom, left* to *right*) two sizes of spring clamps, two sizes of C clamps.

twisting the screw in opposite directions to open or close the parallel wooden jaws.

Another type of clamp is the *C clamp* (called the *G cramp* in England) which also is made in a wide variety of sizes and shapes (Fig. 2.15). It is commonly used to glue parts face-to-face. Openings vary from 2 inches to 12 inches with some C clamps sporting an extra deep throat to afford more working clearance. *Band clamps* or *web clamps* (Fig. 2.15) are used mainly for clamping round or irregular shapes. A beltlike band fits around the area to be held together and a ratchet type of closing is

tightened with a screwdriver as needed. *Steel bar clamps* are used for edge-to-edge gluing where large expanses are involved. Common lengths are from 2 feet to a whopping 10 feet. The final tightening of these clamps is done via a screw-type device. *Spring clamps* are another versatile type, operating like huge clothespins (Fig. 2.15). They are particularly good when quick operations are needed. These clamps quickly spring on or off the parts.

These are but some of a large assortment of clamps. Except, perhaps, when using the wood parallel bar clamps, the wood surfaces to be clamped should

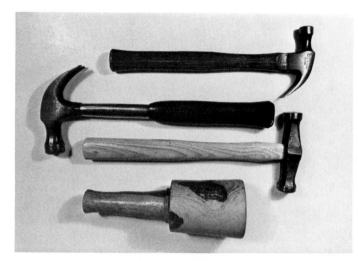

Fig. 2.16 Hammering tools: (from *top*) two claw hammers, doubleheaded hammer, hardwood mallet.

always be protected to prevent the steel ends of the clamps from digging into the wood and marring its surface. Foam rubber, flannel, felt, and even paper towels help to protect surfaces of the wood below the clamp.

ATTACHMENT AIDS

Basic among the attachment aids are tools such as *hammers, mallets, screwdrivers,* and *pliers.* An assortment is shown in Figures 2.16 and 2.17. They are employed directly in operations such as using the screwdriver for attaching screws, and indirectly when the screwdriver is engaged to adjust a tool. Even though they are so universally used for all kinds of materials and needs, there are some specific applications. For one, a mallet, relative to the hammer, is pounded on the head of a chisel or a gouge to drive it.

All these basic tools are manufactured in a wide variety of weights, shapes, and sizes; almost everybody owns at least some of these tools. They have become essential implements for anyone living in a technological society.

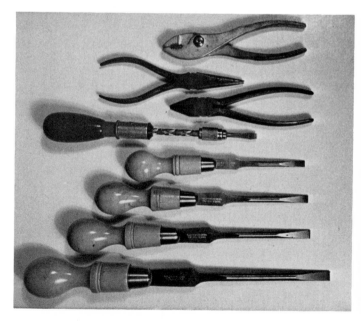

Fig. 2.17 (From *top*) slip-joint pliers, long-nose pliers, cutting pliers, reversible ratchet screwdriver, assorted sizes of standard screwdrivers.

BASIC WOODWORKING OPERATIONS

Along with an understanding about how tools work, we need to know what options are open to us when working with wood. What can we do with the material? What kinds of designs would function best? What range of possibility is there when limited to the basic operations of working with wood, the fundamental processes? (More advanced processes unfold as we progress through the book.)

Basically, we can utilize wood by cutting it, assembling and building up cut pieces, carving solid chunks into new forms, fastening two or more parts together, and bending it. Later on, these aspects expand into more and more variations of cutting, building through lamination, fastening with complex joints, machine carving—which is actually called turning on a lathe—and steam bending of parts. Objects vary from handsome but simple forms, such as trivets, toys, and boxes, to more complex forms such as chairs and cabinets.

No matter what the product will become, there are only three major approaches to working with wood that utilize the basic processes and respect what wood will do. One can build up from flat forms—make constructions. Or one can carve away bits of wood from a solid, reducing it to a final shape. And thirdly, one can combine both these approaches in one object. For instance, flat pieces of wood can be laminated together and, after the wood has been adhered, a form can be carved from that buildup.

The only exception to these principles is to start with a flat shape, steam heat or boil it, then bend the piece of wood into a curve. Once the wood has dried in its bent state, it will remain that way permanently. One may have achieved the same effect by carving the shape from a solid chunk of wood; however, the bending approach is the more economical because there presumably is less waste.

PLANNING A FORM

Since most wood is sold in planks or chunks, at some point it has to be cut to approximate size, and the surface finished roughly by planing it. All of this work can be carried out either with hand tools or with machines. The result is a flat surfaced piece of wood. But all operations do not require straight sides, edges, or parts. Sometimes one wishes to achieve a curved surface. Here is where we carve, cut complex curves,

and mold or bend the wood. Wood turning would be one of the operations employed when one wishes to achieve a curved surface (see Ch. 7). It is possible, nevertheless, to create the same bowl using hand tools as on a wood-turning lathe. In another instance, where thicknesses or colors of wood are not available in the proper sizes, pieces can be glued together into whatever thickness is desired. Whether working with large or small forms, we can laminate thin layers of wood called veneer into thicker chunks, then carve away areas to reveal—as in the strata of the earth seen in cross section—a pattern of different colors and textures of wood. Lamination techniques are covered in Chapter 6.

Design Form and its function are closely related. For example, the shape of a plate would be determined by what use it is to have. Even with design restrictions due to use, variations can be huge.

When beginning, start with drawings or cut pieces of paper that will show what each side will look like—front, back, sides. It is best to play around with pencil and paper, rather than attacking the wood directly, particularly when one begins to work with wood. Errors can be costly in terms of time and materials.

It is very difficult to say with certainty why one shape succeeds and another one fails. There are no hard and fast rules. It takes experienced looking to be able to make qualitative distinctions.

If any rule can be established, however, it would be one tilting toward a preference for simple forms.

When planning, think from the general to the particular and work the same way. Don't get caught up with surface details but consider the overall shape first. Details come later. There is one consideration of surface, however, that comes into play when planning and that is the pattern formed by the grain of the wood. Try to let the pattern of the wood help to guide what the eventual shape will become. At the very least, do not fight the grain pattern of the wood, particularly when the grain is dominant. The material provides the message as to what the shape will be. This is almost as important as the consideration of how the piece will be used; how it will function. Above all, remember that you are working with wood. The final object should look like wood, not metal or ceramic. Respect what can be done with wood and don't try to design a wood form the same way you would design a shape for metal.

Contours and Templates After looking at many forms that you think are successful, try your hand at one you invent yourself. Cut paper shapes (contours) and tape them to the sides of the wood. Study the relationships of sizes and shapes. Try to visualize what the piece will look like when excess wood is cut away. If one part does not succeed, adjust the outlines. Eventually these shapes or contours will become templates for you to trace around. Areas to

be cut away can be marked with an "X." All professionals use templates.

When you are certain that the form, its function, and the wood are compatible, lightly outline the shapes to be cut away directly onto the wood with a pencil. Try to use the best surfaces of the wood. If the wood is to be planed, all measurements should be general (a bit larger) for the first cutting, allowing for more wood to be planed away so there is no extreme roughness or warped area. Then, before assembling, pieces have to be accurately cut. All cuts should be performed on the outside of the pencil mark.

FUNDAMENTAL SKILLS

Figures 3.1 through 3.12 illustrate some basic operations, the minimal skills necessary to create simple forms. Following this "basic operations vocabulary" are some more specific procedures that build upon the basic operations while simultaneously exploring the potential of wood.

Cutting Shapes It is possible to create well-designed forms and be very inventive by just cutting, sanding, and finishing wood. No assembly or joining operations need be involved. At its simplest, only a single piece of wood is used. Figure 3.13 illustrates the making of a picture puzzle from a single piece.

Using a board or block of wood and performing various cutting operations, one can create puzzles, pencil holders,

Fig. 3.1 The marking gauge is used to mark off guide-lines parallel to an edge, end, or surface of a piece of wood. It has a sharp spur or pin that does the marking. To draw a line parallel to an edge, first determine the distance and adjust the gauge by setting the head (accomplished by loosening the screw). Press the head firmly against the edge of the work and with a wrist motion, tip the gauge forward until the spur touches the work. Bear down now so the spur marks the wood.

Fig. 3.2 Dividers are useful for transferring measurements or inscribing arcs and circles. To lay out a circle, set the divider at the desired radius. Place one leg of the divider at the center of the proposed circle, lean the tool in the direction it will be rotated, and rotate it by twisting it between thumb and forefinger.

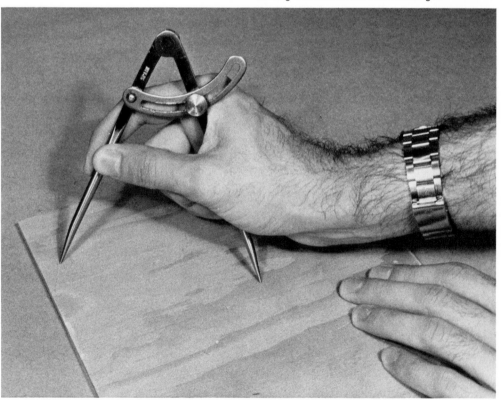

key holders, mirrors, bookends and sculptures. Several examples are shown in Figures 3.14 through 3.18.

Curling and Bending Wood Thin wood, available as veneers and in strips as shelf edging, can be soaked in water, then curled and/or bent into shape. The basic operations are learning how to cut veneers and how to shape them when wet, procedures shown in Figures 3.19 and 3.20.

Floral forms, ornaments and decorations, mobile elements, and sculptures are just a few of the possibilities attainable through the use of curling and bending wood veneers and strips. Figures 3.21 through 3.23 show some creative applications.

Joining and Gluing Wood The longest lasting and most attractive way to join wood is to cut joints into the wood, then adhere the joint parts with an adhesive. The least satisfactory way to join wood is through use of fasteners, such as nails and screws.

There are many types of joints. Diagrams of some of the more popular and frequently used joints are shown in Figure 3.24. Certain ways of joining wood are more often employed for particular projects. For example, varieties of *dovetail joints* are most commonly used for drawers.

Doweled joints are utilized to reinforce butt joining in frame-type projects (a *butt joint* or *plain joint* is the square end of one piece fitting against the flat surface of another piece).

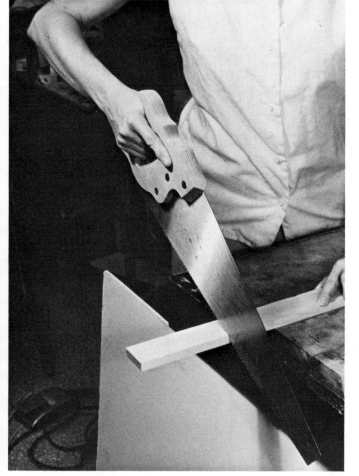

Fig. 3.3 The crosscut saw is employed for cutting across the grain. Place the board to be cut on a stationary object. Hold the saw so that the first finger extends along the handle. Grasp the board with the other hand so that it remains rigid. The side of the saw should be at a right angle to the face of the board and the cutting angle at about 45° to the face of the board. To begin, take short, light strokes, gradually increasing them to the full length of the saw. The arm that does the sawing should swing clear of your body. If the saw sticks or binds, it is because the saw may be dull or the wood may have too much moisture in it. Use some candle wax on your saw. Keep your eye on the line when sawing, not on the saw.

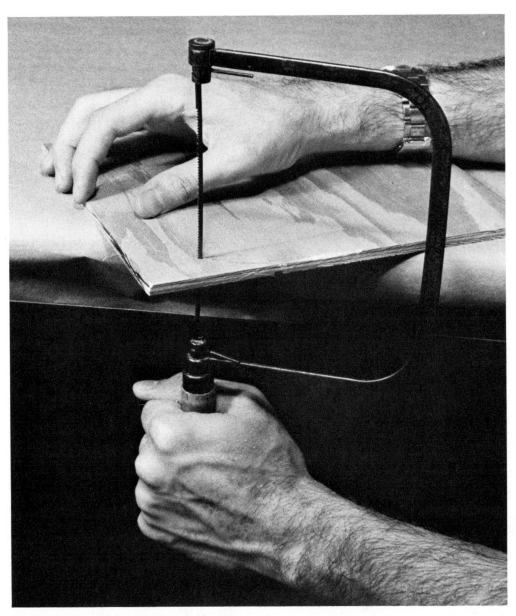

Fig. 3.4 A coping saw is used to cut along curved lines where fine detail is needed. The blade should be positioned at a right angle to the face of the wood. Use forward pressure and cut away from your body. For inside cuts, drill a hole in the wood, thread the saw blade through the hole, then reattach the blade to the coping saw frame.

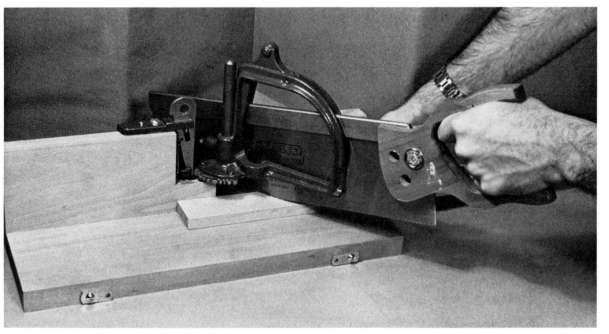

Fig. 3.5 One use for a back saw is to cut miters within a miter box. It is also a crosscut saw designed to cut a straight line across the face of a piece of stock. When cutting a miter using a miter box, set the saw within the guide and draw the saw at first with short strokes, then with longer strokes.

When *mitered corners,* such as those used in the making of display trays, are used, feathers or keys (triangular pieces of wood) are inserted in parallel formation into the mitered corner.

Various types of *mortise and tenon joints* are often found in the joining of furniture legs for chairs and tables.

Step by step construction of a pine trivet joined entirely with cross lap joints is shown in Figure 3.25.

Figures 3.26 through 3.31 illustrate the selection of the most appropriate joints for specific projects.

There are two types of adhesives that work best when adhering wood joints. One is Weldwood, a plastic resin that comes in powdered form and requires mixing with a small amount of water. White glues, such as polyvinyl chloride and polyvinyl acetate with brand names such as Elmer's and Sobo, provide an alternative. However, of the two types, Weldwood adheres best.

Two-part epoxies are also good and are applied in some operations, as well as other plastic resin glues that can be used with good results.

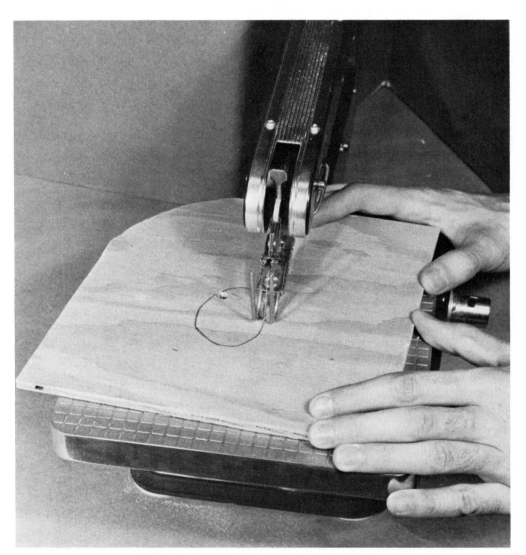

Fig. 3.6 A scroll saw or jigsaw, such as this Dremel
Moto-Saw, is utilized to cut curves and circles from
interior sections, as well as for fine cutting. To cut a
circle in the center of a piece of wood, drill a hole; dis-
engage the saw blade and thread the blade through the
hole, then reattach it. The cutting edge of the blade is
toward you. In this cutting action, therefore, the wood
moves away from you toward the arm of the saw.

Fig. 3.7 The band saw can be equipped with different widths of blades (*see* Ch. 2). Straight lines and curves can be cut with the band saw. A fence or jig is usually used, as in this case, to guide the cut.

Fig. 3.8 A table saw, with its fence adjusted to the proper width, is used to make straight cuts. Hands should be kept well away from the blade using a pusher, as shown in Figure 3.9.

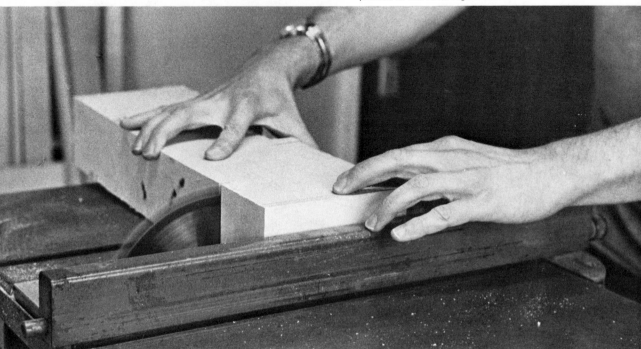

Fig. 3.9 Note the chewed edges of the center pusher—it certainly took the risk out of cutting.

Fig. 3.10 The drill press is used primarily to drill holes of various dimensions (Dremel makes a hobby-type drill press adequate for small work). When operating a drill press, make certain that the bit is properly secured in the chuck. Do not remove work from the table until the drill has completely stopped. Here an expansive bit is being used to cut a wide hole. The largest expansive bit has three cutters and bores holes up to 4 inches in diameter. Note that the work is securely braced with C clamps.

Fig. 3.11 Router bits are capable of delivering the power to cut internal patterns in wood, as for this lap joint. Different depths are achieved by adjusting the height of the cutter. Movement is from the right toward the left, when a hand-held router is table mounted. Using various contours of router bits, moldings, trims, edges, and complex contours can be cut.

Fig. 3.12 Drum sanders (as shown here), belt sanders, and disk sanders refine the final contours and deliver a finished surface. In this case, the work is moved over the rotating sanding drum. When using hand-held sanding devices, the work remains stationary while the sanding tool is kept in constant motion.

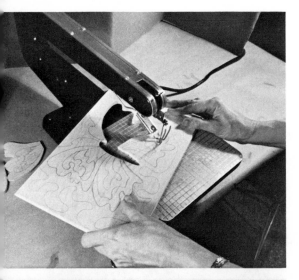

Fig. 3.13a A jigsaw is used to cut a jigsaw puzzle. Parts are outlined on the board first. The back is marked to distinguish it from the front.

Fig. 3.13b Selected top surfaces are painted with acrylic paint.

Fig. 3.13c The decorative 8 by 10-inch puzzle, made by the author, is also shown in Figure 10 in the color section.

Fig. 3.14 William Accorsi's sculpture, 5 inches tall, is also shown in color, Figure 1. The parts fit together as in a three-dimensional puzzle.

Fig. 3.15 A puzzle painting in wood, 39 inches high, by Kari Lonning.

Utilizing Scrap Pieces One can save or gather scrap pieces of wood. Bags full of scraps can be purchased from woodworkers or lumber yards. It is an economical and simple way to begin.

The skills involved are sanding, gluing, and finishing operations. Most important, though, is the study of how pieces can relate to one another. The negative and positive spaces are created as one shape is placed next to another shape. Use of thicker or deeper forms and inclusion of thinner forms establish still another dimension: the shadow patterns cast by the deeper shapes upon the shallower shapes.

Working with scrap pieces has much potential. Door and drawer fronts can be patterned this way. Cocktail tables can be made from scraps and topped with

Fig. 3.16 Cutting, sanding, and ingenuity went into this keyboard by Joyce and Edgar Anderson. Keys are attached to wooden disks, which in turn slide into grooves in the main panel, which is 15 inches high.

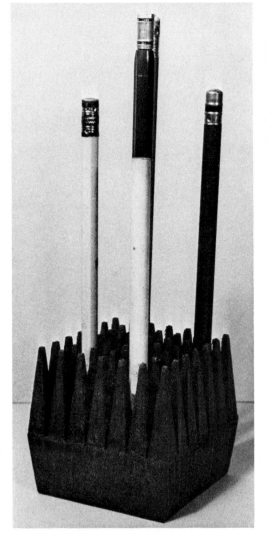

Fig. 3.17 A pencil holder made from a 2¼-inch cube by cutting away triangular sections.

Fig. 3.18 A mirror is fitted into a cavity that was routed out of a block of wood. Made by John Makepeace, it stands 4½ inches high.

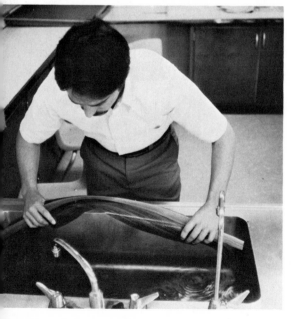

Fig. 3.19a Bob Ciscell soaked a piece of veneer in hot water. Here he is testing it for pliability.

Fig. 3.19b While the wood is wet and hot, it remains flexible enough to bend, clip together, and staple temporarily while the form drys and hardens. Parts that touch one another are then glued with a white glue.

Fig. 3.19c The piece is curved, wrapped around, and attached only at a few points. Clear shellac or varnish is used as a finish. This veneer sculpture was made from discarded production scraps and sample sheets and stands 22 inches high. "Mother/Child" by Bob Ciscell; also shown in color, Figure 4. *Courtesy: Bob Ciscell*

Fig. 3.20a This is veneer shelf edging that can be purchased in most lumber supply and hardware stores. A veneer saw is being used to cut, but scissors also perform well for this thickness of veneer.

Fig. 3.20b The veneer is soaked for about 10 minutes in hot water, then is immediately wrapped around a wooden dowel. Parts are clipped in place until they dry and maintain their forms.

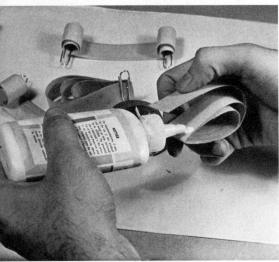

Fig. 3.20c Then edges are glued with a white glue such as Tite-Bond or Elmer's. . .

Fig. 3.20d . . . and are held with paper clips again until the glue dries.

Fig. 3.20e Parts are assembled using paper clips again and the glue is allowed to harden.

Fig. 3.20f The completed veneer butterfly.

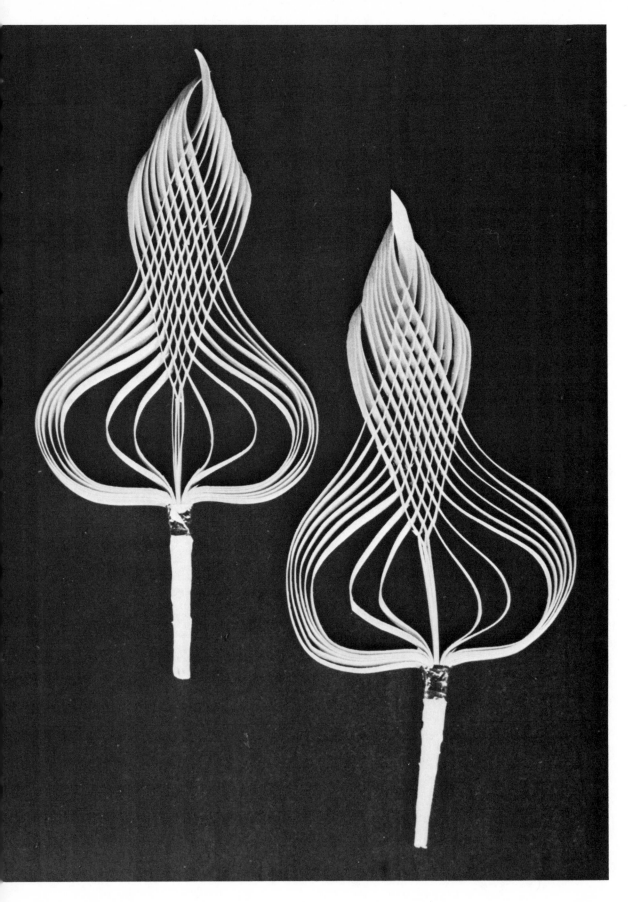

Fig. 3.21 A holiday ornament from Japan made with pine veneer. No glue is used. Cross lap joints are used and the whole is wrapped at the stem with paper.

Fig. 3.22 Flowers from Finland made from thin pine shavings. Some were colored with aniline dye before bending.

Fig. 3.23 A closeup of the flowers in Figure 3.22. Stems were made of wire and wrapped with paper. And parts were attached with white glue.

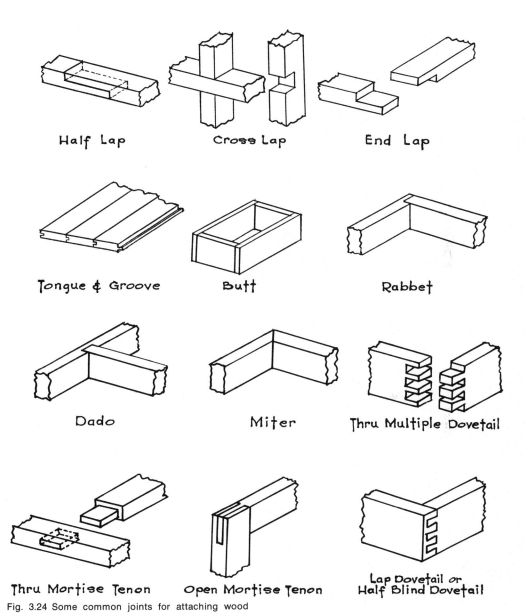

Half Lap   Cross Lap   End Lap

Tongue & Groove   Butt   Rabbet

Dado   Miter   Thru Multiple Dovetail

Thru Mortise Tenon   Open Mortise Tenon   Lap Dovetail or Half Blind Dovetail

Fig. 3.24 Some common joints for attaching wood parts. *Courtesy: Stanley Tools*

Fig. 3.25a Cross lap joints are used to make a trivet of pine. The cross cuts are sliced into thin strips of wood.

Fig. 3.25b Then the cut pieces are chiseled out to form one part of the base.

Fig. 3.25c Weldwood glue is mixed and applied at the joints. The parts are then clamped.

Fig. 3.25d While the glue is setting, strips of pine are cut into squares using a radial arm saw. A jig is used to gauge the width of pieces for cutting. Edges are sanded smooth.

Fig. 3.25e At each juncture a drop of glue is added and . . .

Fig. 3.25f . . . a block is carefully placed over each spot of glue. Each block is arranged so that the grain of the blocks alternates, horizontally and vertically, and spaces are evenly maintained between pieces.

Fig. 3.25g The completed trivet. A coating of urethane varnish provides a protective finish.

glass. Bookends, scrapbook covers, panels, and sculptures can also be made by gluing found forms of wood onto a surface. Figure 3.32 shows the procedural sequence for making a lamp from scrap wood. Figures 3.33 and 3.34 illustrate interesting uses of small pieces of wood.

Joints That Articulate Movable parts can be made by using string, elastic, or wire to thread parts together. The new skill required here is drilling parts so that they can be strung. Since the life of this joint depends upon the wear and tear of the material used for stringing the parts, it cannot be considered the strongest or longest lasting joint. Nevertheless, toys and even box hinges

sometimes are made with nylon or cotton string.

The photographic sequence in Figure 3.35 shows the steps for assembling a toy snake using nylon thread. The toys in Figure 3.36 have movable joints assembled with brad nails, rather than threaded.

FINISHING TECHNIQUES

When any work of forming objects of wood has been completed, the final operation with wood is the finishing process—whether wood will be sanded and what kind of coating will protect the surface. Unless the wood's natural surface is unattractive or nondescript, it is

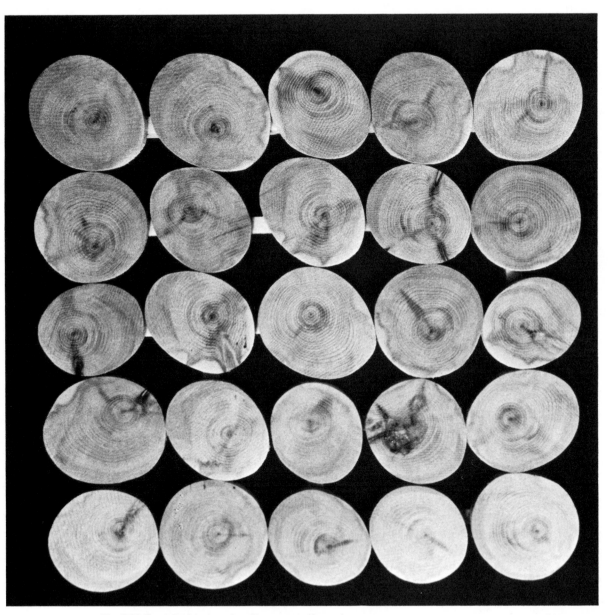

Fig. 3.26 Top of a trivet made with cross sections of birch. Edges are trimmed and the surface finely sanded. The base was constructed the same way as the pine trivet (Fig. 3.25).

Fig. 3.27 A butter box made of birch bark and birch wood from Lapland. No glue or metal was utilized to fasten parts: only pegs were used, so tightly fitted that this 30-year-old piece is still as precisely joined as when it was new.

usually advisable to use transparent stains and finishes. These will allow the essence of "woodness," the quality of wood, to show through.

Sanding The kind of work that is done will dictate whether and how much sanding should be done. Some pieces depend upon texturing done with a tool

to provide an aspect of its design. In that case, sanding would obliterate that quality and is undesirable. Other styles look better with a slick, finely sanded surface.

Sanding can be refined down from #80 garnet open-coat paper or Corosil paper (tougher than garnet), all the way to #220 or #400. Further surface finishing can be accomplished with #0000 steel wool. After sanding, dust is wiped off the wood with Tack-Cloth—a waxy cloth to which sawdust sticks—before applying the protective finish. Otherwise, the dust will mix with the finish and impart a gritty texture.

Transparent Stains If one feels it is necessary to stain or color the wood,

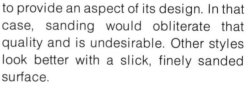

Fig. 3.28 The inside and lid of the butter box in Figure 3.27, showing the exact fitting of sides and handle.

Fig. 3.29 Two hangers from Sweden: parts were joined
with closed mortise tenon joints.

Fig. 3.30 A wine rack by Irving Fischman, assembled by a decorative version of thru mortise tenon joints (also shown in color section, Fig. 12).

several kinds of transparent stains are available.

Water stains are water soluble. They should not be used on tool-marked surfaces or on pieces where end grain is predominant. They tend to raise the grain and look spotty. Of the water dyes, fabric dyes can be used, but these colors are less permanent.

Alcohol stains: the non-grain raising (NGR) types are easy to apply and are fast drying, but can leave a blotchy look if there are any soft spots in the wood.

These are among the more permanent stains.

Oil stains provide an even coating. They consist of dyes that are dissolved in oil. They tend to be somewhat less permanent than the alcohol types.

Pigmented wiping stains are diluted paint products that are available as oil-based or water-based materials. They are applied as the others by brushing or wiping on with a soft cloth.

Penetration of any of the stains can be controlled, particularly with end-grained

Fig. 3.31 "Noah's Ark," made of oak and cedar with maple figures by the Rochester Folk Art Guild. Acrylic colors are used to paint characteristic patterns on the figures, which were cut on a jigsaw. In most cases the paint doesn't totally cover the figure and the grain of the wood is permitted to show through. *Courtesy: Rochester Folk Art Guild*

Fig. 3.32a Scrap pieces of walnut were salvaged to make a lamp. Edges are sanded and pieces are then arranged on portable aluminum trays. Weldwood plastic resin glue is measured with a dry teaspoon and a small amount of water added; the two are mixed until a paste-like consistency is reached (moisture or excessive heat will degrade this resin).

Fig. 3.32b The glue is brushed onto edges that are to be joined.

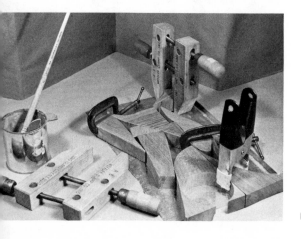

Fig. 3.32c Parts are then clamped until the glue sets.

Fig. 3.32d After the glue has set, the clamps are removed. On the left are some scrap pieces similar to those used to form the lamp base.

Fig. 3.32e The glued-up panels are attached to a walnut base. Holes are drilled for screw attachment, then the pieces are glued at contact points as well.

Fig. 3.32f The completed lamp has an acrylic box behind the wood panels. Lamp attachments feed through the acrylic box, and through and under the walnut base, where they are attached.

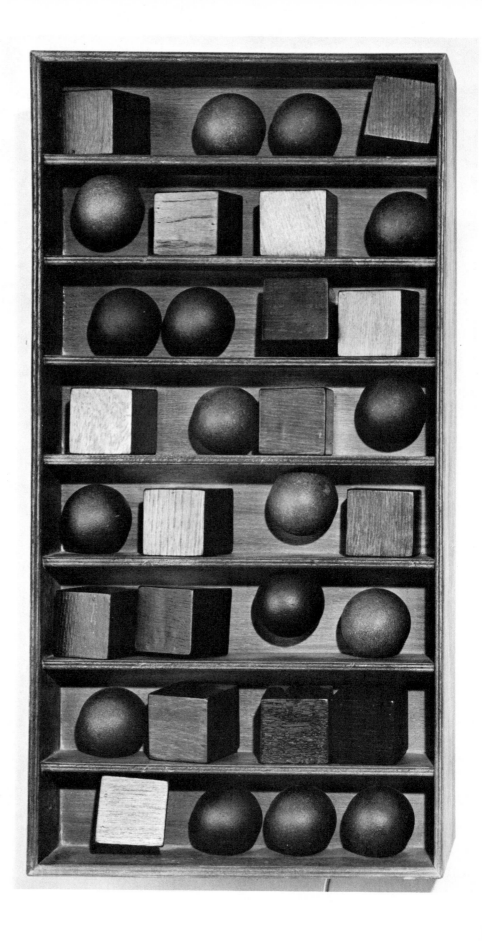

Fig. 3.33 Pol Bury's "16 Balls, 16 Cubes on 7 Shelves,"
1966. *Courtesy: The Tate Gallery, London*

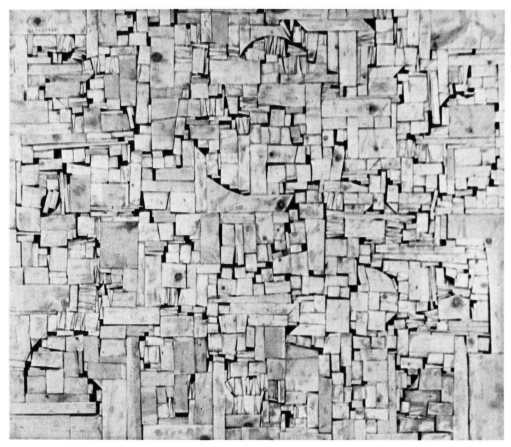

Fig. 3.34 A wood relief made from scraps of pine. The
pieces were kept in natural color and the background
was painted blue. By Bernard Langlais, "Plan with
Blue," 68 by 81 inches, 1960. *Courtesy: Bernard
Langlais, Allan Stone Collection*

wood, by applying a dilute solution of
shellac (dilute with alcohol) before
staining.

Clear Finishes Before applying any
clear finish, use a Tack-Cloth to remove
dust. Of the clear finishes, boiled linseed oil or similar oils such as teak are a
most satisfactory finish. Oil can be
wiped on as it comes from the can, or
heated to about 80°F (slightly warmer
than room temperature) and applied.
The procedure is to apply the oil with a
brush or rag; allow it to soak in. Wipe the
surface free of oil and reapply coats
several times more that day, then once a
week for a month. Each time, dry and
rub the surface. Be certain to read the

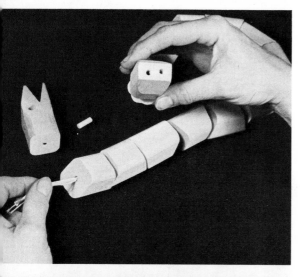

Fig. 3.35a Pieces for the snake toy are cut and sharp edges sanded to round them a bit. A single hole is drilled in the center of each piece of wood—except for the end of the tail, which has two holes.

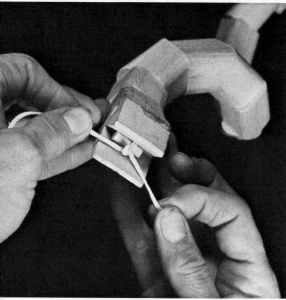

Fig. 3.35b All thread ends are strung through the single hole in the head, down through each piece to the tail, then back through the same holes. The threads are tied once and wrapped around a small piece of dowel, pulled tightly and tied again.

product instructions, paying special heed to any precautions about flammability of oils when heating.

Another very simple clear finish to apply is *petroleum jelly*. It imparts a silky appearance and does not leave a greasy surface, as one might expect. It is applied with a soft cloth; excess is wiped off after penetration.

For forms such as bowls, trays, goblets—anything that will contain food—nonpoisonous finishes are imperative. Of the most commonly available,

melted beeswax that has been thinned with a bit of *mineral oil* is best. The mixture is applied hot (at temperature at which wax melts) with a soft cloth.

Olive oil and *salad oil* are also good for wooden kitchen utensils. These oils should be used periodically. Wash and dry such food utensils and containers quickly after they are used to keep the wood from swelling and cracking.

There also are some special *varnishes* compounded for wooden food containers that will be used for alkaline

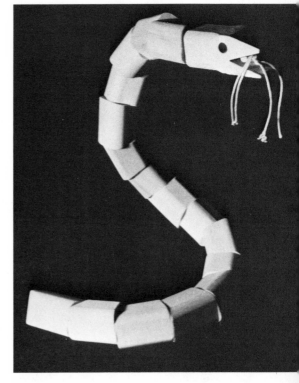

Fig. 3.35c The completed snake can be articulated into many shapes. If the snake doesn't hold its shape, then the nylon string has to be pulled more tightly.

Fig. 3.36 Toys from Sweden made of laminated pine. Arms, heads, and legs move on pins which are brad nails—equipped with heads that are embedded and glued in the body.

or acid foods. These are available from mail-order houses that specialize in products for the woodworker (*see* Sources of Supply).

Another kind of wax is hard *carnauba wax* used for floors. Heat the wax until it melts and apply it with a brush in a warm room to allow the wax to penetrate. Wait an hour before buffing with a clean shoeshine brush.

Shellac is one of the oldest and most satisfactory finishes for wood. It should be used when fresh (don't try to store it) and applied on a dry day, since moisture adversely affects its properties. Cut the shellac with some alcohol by mixing about four parts of alcohol to three parts of three-pound cut shellac, or three parts of alcohol to one part of four-pound cut shellac. Shellac is usually brushed on. Allow each coat to dry thoroughly before applying the next coat. Sanding between coats improves the final finish, but don't forget to clear away residue with Tack-Cloth.

There are a great many, very good *plastic-based varnishes* on the market that provide excellent finishes where weather, wear, and abrasion are factors in the use of a product. They are applied by brush the same way as shellac. Follow instructions on the can. Some should be stirred and others should not. Solvents for these synthetic varnishes vary.

BASIC CONSTRUCTION: MAKING A BOX

Perhaps the best way to describe basic construction techniques is to bring you through the actual process of making a basic box, starting from scratch and using frame and panel construction. Through step by step photographs and captions, you can see the operations described visually as well as verbally. Before this sequence of making a box begins, let us look at a few preliminaries.

DESIGN AND MATERIALS

Prior to any construction, you must have a design for what is to be made, templates to act as cutting guides, and a list of all pieces of wood and sizes that you will need. Then the best wood available should be on hand, as well as a plan of action. In what order are parts to be cut? What kinds of joining will be required? In what order will elements be assembled?

What kind of finish will be used on the wood? These are significant questions, answers to which will avoid costly errors later on. You must think through all steps, else you may find that you have completed a great deal of work and the parts cannot be assembled because something was glued up beforehand and is in the way.

Many of the operations shown here are performed by machines in a woodworking shop. Each step, however, can be carried out by hand, as it has been done for centuries. It just takes more time. The sequence of steps and procedures is essentially the same.

CONSTRUCTING THE PARTS

Cutting First, the wood has to be cut to approximate size. All measurements should be checked and double checked throughout the processes. At least a 1/4-inch (6mm) allowance should be made on the width, 1/2 inch (12mm) on the length, and 3/32 inch (2.5mm) on the thickness. This will permit squaring and the elimination of any slight warpage.

The wood is then rip-sawed along the grain for one measurement, and crosscut across the grain for the other dimension. Corners should be right angles if square cuts are desired, as in the box. When cutting with either saw, do so in a leisurely fashion and try to cut, not for speed, but for accuracy. Solid paraffin (candle wax) is a good lubricant for the saw blade. It helps to minimize friction.

At this point, if a board has been sliced in half of its thickness, some woodworkers recommend letting the wood sit for a few days to let parts stabilize to conditions. When tensions in the wood have been released through cutting, the wood has a tendency to warp. After this bit of seasoning, the wood can then be cut to exact measurements by repeating most of the previous operations. Figure 4.1 illustrates the step by step procedures for cutting to approximate dimensions, then refining cuts to precise measurements.

Fig. 4.1a After a preliminary design and list of parts, a plan of action has been worked out. Wood is brought down to slightly *larger* than final size by cutting pieces on the band saw.

Fig. 4.1b Sides are planed with a jack plane until straight and true.

Fig. 4.1c Edges are planed in the same manner as the sides.

Fig. 4.1d Again using a band saw, nearly the proper width is obtained by slicing the thickness of a board, allowing for some cutting later. Note the use of a pusher so that fingers are kept away from the saw blade.

Fig. 4.1e After all of this cutting, new surfaces are now exposed to air, so the wood is left to stabilize or season for a few days. The wood is going to warp.

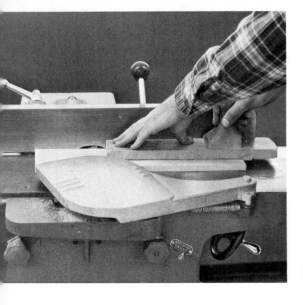

Fig. 4.1f After seasoning, the wood is edged in a joiner to achieve a straight side.

Fig. 4.1g Then the board is planed on both sides to the proper size.

Fig. 4.1h A final edge is established on the joiner.

Fig. 4.1i The boards are sawed to final width, then rip-sawed to exact height. By flipping the board over to get square edges, there are now four pieces of wood, each with six square flat surfaces.

Planing Now that parts are cut, a jack plane can be used for leveling and smoothing the parts. The cutting iron of the plane should be set so that a continuous curl issues forth as the plane is moved. If the plane digs in, the cutting iron should be readjusted. A bit of paraffin on the sole of the plane helps to cut down friction here, too. All sides of the wood parts need to be planed. You can check to see whether sides are true (straight) by placing a straight edge on the surface. If there are valleys and hills, then continue the planing operation. In some instances, it might be more expedient to have the boards planed to size at the lumber yard or in a woodworking shop.

Forming Joints Now that the surfaces are flat and smooth, the edges are squared, and the sizes are accurate, you will want to mark off the joints. The photographic series in Figure 4.2 illus-

Fig. 4.2a With a marking gauge, the depth of the dovetail is established.

Fig. 4.2b The design of the dovetail is sketched out.

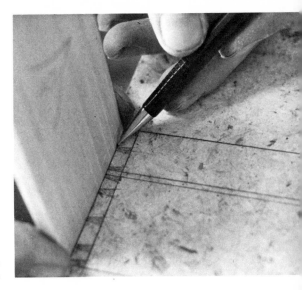

Fig. 4.2c The lines for the dovetail are transferred to the edge of a board. The tails are marked and cut first.

Fig. 4.2d A dovetail marking jig is used to trace off the angle of the dovetail, following the pattern of the original drawing. This is done for four corners. Parts to be cut away are colored in so there is no confusion as to which part to cut.

Fig. 4.2e Using a dovetail saw, the downward cuts are sawed to the guideline.

Fig. 4.2f A block is set up at the edge of the guideline and clamped. This is to keep the chisel from backing up as it is hit. The chisel tends to step backwards.

Fig. 4.2g With the flat of the chisel touching the block, the chisel is hit with a mallet so that the chisel blade cuts across the fibers at the guideline.

Fig. 4.2h Here the chisel is hit into the end grain to chop out a piece. The process continues until all tails are formed.

Fig. 4.2i Use a knife to trace the tails onto the end of the adjoining piece, which is in a vertical position, for the pins. These marks indicate where the saw is to cut. The next slices are made straight down to the guideline. The pins are now chiseled out, the same way as the tails. Very little trimming is necessary. Dovetail joints should not be tested all the way because they are designed for a tight fit and should not come apart.

trates each procedure for making dovetail joints, commonly used for boxes and drawers. The dovetail for the box shown in the construction sequence was designed and drawn on the corner of the woodworking bench—although paper, wood, or anything will do. From your drawing, the dovetails are marked directly onto the wood being used. And a line is scribed around all three sides. The areas to be eliminated are marked as well. Sometimes the distinction between what to cut and what not to remove is difficult when cutting. A homemade marking jig helps establish uniform angles for the dovetails.

Then, while the piece is held in a vise, with a dovetail saw, all the lines leading from the edge are cut. After that, the chisel is hit down on the adjacent line and the negative space—the *tail*—is cut away. A block clamped against the line keeps the chisel from jumping too far over the line in the wrong direction.

Next, small layers of the end grain are hit, chipping out pieces. This continues until all the tails are cut out. Then, using this piece as a guide, the tails are marked onto the piece to be joined. These parts will become the *pins*. In order to mark the pins, one board is set down on top of the other and a sharp knife is used to outline the shapes. After the marking operation, the procedure is the same as that for making of the tails. Usually there is a slight bit of trimming to do here and there. So, you chisel away the parts that you have missed, taking care not to cut away too much and ruin the joint. To judge a fit, just tap parts together.

If any grooves are to be made in the piece for inside fittings or dividers, and panels for the top and bottom of this frame and panel construction, they should be routed or chiseled out now. A jig should be used, in either case, to maintain the position of the groove and help control the direction of the tool. The parts to be used for dividers should be available to gauge the thickness of the groove. Figure 4.3 shows the steps involved in making the grooves.

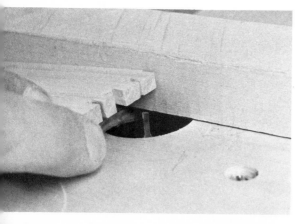

Fig. 4.3a After setting a jig for the #24 router and adjusting the height of the bit so that the proper depth is reached, grooves are cut along the top and bottom edges of the sides so that the top and bottom panels can be inserted into the frame formed by the four sides.

Fig. 4.3b Next, with a jig equipped with stops, the sides of the box are prepared for routing out grooves to be used to hold the dividers. The jig is screwed into the table to clamp down the wood.

Fig. 4.3c This shows the router used this time from the top, with the jig in place.

Fig. 4.3d The grooves are routed out now. To do this the router is placed in position, turned on, and the rotating bit is lowered into the wood.

Fig. 4.4 Now there are four sides of the box, with dove-tails cut, and grooves cut for the panel and dividers. The interior portions of the box are finished off by sanding and the edges are chamfered with a file.

Chamfering and Oiling Now four sides of the box are cut, as well as the approximate sizes of the dividers; grooves are cut into the box for the dividers and panels; edges to be joined have been cut to contain tails and pins. Some finishing operations start here, particularly for the inside of the box—even before gluing. It certainly is easier to sand a flat piece rather than an interior corner space (Fig. 4.4).

For a finer touch in finishing, the edges are chamfered all around the inside edge and for the dividers. *Chamfering* is the cutting of a slight bevel into an edge. It helps to define the edge more. Chamfering is accomplished with a file.

Then masking tape is placed on the joints and the parts are oiled (Fig. 4.5). The masking tape prevents the joints from getting oil on them, which would

Fig. 4.5 The edges that are to be glued and the rest of the inside of the box is oiled. Oiling at this point is an optional approach.

inhibit gluing. Oiling can be accomplished, as well, after the entire box has been glued and assembled. Oiling before assembly keeps glue that may ooze out from filling the wood pores—which would later keep the oil from penetrating.

ASSEMBLING THE BOX

Tongue and Groove A tongue is formed on the panel parts (top and bottom of the box) using a shaper-cutter, as shown in Figure 4.6. The tongue will slide into the grooves previously cut in the sides, allowing a fraction of leeway for the panel to expand and contract. For parts that are small, a file or a chisel will do the job of shaping the tongue or groove. The panels are fitted tongue into groove and the dividers are fitted to accurate size. It is preferable to have the top of the panel fit flush with the top edge of the sides; less interior space is lost this way.

Fig. 4.6 The top and bottom panels have been cut to size in the same manner as the sides of the box. Here the tongue is being made with a three-ring shaper-cutter. The end result is a chamfered edge that is the same thickness as the grooves that were cut in the sides. With the tongue cut, the panel will just slip into the groove.

Fig. 4.7 Now all parts have been cut, sanded, and oiled and the dividers are assembled. Note that dowels are used to pin or position the dividers on the box interior, making for easy assembly. This clearly shows a frame and panel construction.

Frame and Panel Now all parts are ready to be assembled (Fig. 4.7). The two end pieces and one long side are assembled and their dovetail joints are glued. The other long side is left off so that the dividers can be placed in the box.

The top and bottom panels are now fitted—but not glued—into place within the three-sided frame.

The fourth side of the box, the part that was left open to allow for the insertion of the top and bottom panels, is glued into place after the dividers have been positioned by doweling (see Fig. 4.7) and glued.

Making the Opening Now you have a box that does not open, with an interior that is blind. Parallel marks are drawn with pencil on the sides of the box frame where the box is to open, then the piece is sawed apart, as shown in Figure 4.8. In this case, a table saw is used. But with jigs set up and clamped in place, the box can be cut apart to form the lid and base of the box with a handsaw.

For a more accurate and clean cut when utilizing a table saw, the saw should be set so that the blade does not go all the way through to separate lid from base. The blade just forms a groove. Then a handsaw is used to finish the cut. The result is cleaner.

Finishing Touches Finally, if hardware is to be used, it is attached at this point. Hinges are recessed by slicing the box to the depth or thickness of the hinge. The area is then chiseled away. Top and bottom are aligned and, with a drill marked with masking tape to indicate the depth of the drill hole, holes are made where screws are to be inserted. The photographic series in Figure 4.9 illustrates the steps.

Final planing, sanding, or finishing around the edges that have been cut completes the making of the box (Fig. 4.10).

Fig. 4.8a Edges to be attached are glued and the entire box is assembled. Everything inside is blind because at this point the box cannot be opened.

Fig. 4.8b The "opening" for the lid of the box is marked, taking into account the height of the dividers and allowing for the saw blade thickness—how much is to be lost in cutting. That is why planning is so important. Every aspect has to be considered beforehand.

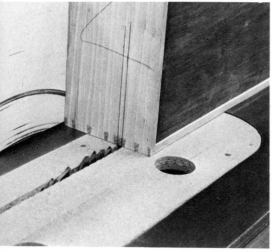

Fig. 4.8c With the fence and saw height adjusted, the box is run through the table saw, but not quite all the way through the thickness of the wood. This is to keep the box from opening up and falling into the saw when the final side is cut. After all sides have been cut, what is seen is a groove running all around the box. Then, with a hand saw, the last bit is sawed. The resulting burr is filed or planed away. The box now has a lid and base.

Fig. 4.9a In preparation for the hinges, a dovetail saw is used to cut down across the grain. Two cuts are made for the outside width of the hinge.

Fig. 4.9b A chisel is used to cut away enough wood to accommodate for the thickness of the hinge.

Fig. 4.9c Excess is trimmed away.

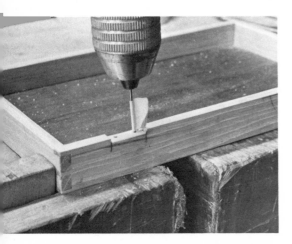

Fig. 4.9d Masking tape is placed on a twist drill bit to indicate the depth of the hole and holes are drilled for screws.

Fig. 4.9e Hinges are now attached with screwdriver and screws. An interior catch is added that operates on inward pressure of a dowel and small spring.

Fig. 4.10 The box is then very lightly planed to clean
off the sides and it is completed by sanding and oiling.

Fig. 4.11 The interior of the completed box.

Fig. 4.12 The box as it looks closed. The top and bottom are walnut and the sides are bitternut hickory.
Photos by Robert Sperber, Box by Robert Sperber

Fig. 4.13 A walnut-topped box with a unique lid by Joyce Anderson.

At this point additional, or first time, oiling of the finish is done (see Ch. 3). Linseed oil applied with a soft rag was used to finish this box. The interior of the completed box, which was designed and made by Robert Sperber, is shown in Figure 4.11; the finished exterior is shown in Figure 4.12. An unusual box by another artist is shown in Figure 4.13.

TEXTURING AND CARVING

The surface of wood can be textured, designed, or altered for its own sake, as in shallow carvings and slightly deeper bas relief, or textured as a change of surface, or to dramatize an uninteresting grain. Or these techniques can be used for wood that is a part of something else, such as the lid of a box or within the panel of a cabinet door. These kinds of carvings have been done for centuries, with variations that reflect the images of the age.

TEXTURING

With Tools Texturing can be accomplished by means of sandpaper—sanding the surface until the desired roughness or smoothness has been achieved. Or one can employ Surform tools which contain tiny razor-sharp perforations that grate away small areas of wood (*see* Fig. 2.7). Other abrading tools such as steel *rasps,* which are coarse files, or *rifflers,* which are small curved files or rasps and

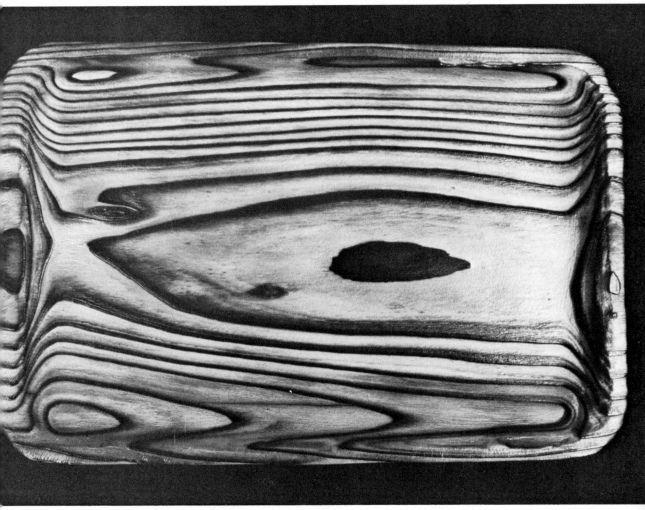

Fig. 5.1 Flame was used to texture the wood of this tray from Japan, 14 inches wide. Charred areas are wire-brushed away, resulting in a contrast of darks and lights with predominant grain figure patterning the surface.

scrapers, also slowly cut away the wood's surface while leaving the characteristic mark of the instrument.

Deeper patterns are left by knives, chisels, and carving tools. By cutting at an angle, light and shadow-catching patterns can be achieved, as in chip carving and incising. The larger the form or area to be cut, the larger the tool that is used. To carve away large chunks in rough-hewn textures, the *adz* is one of the oldest instruments used by man. This is a hatchetlike tool that chops away chunks of wood. They vary in size

from small cutting heads to large cutting heads.

With Heat and Flame The grain of some woods, such as pine, limewood, larch, and ash, can be dramatized and made more pronounced by slightly charring or burning the surface (Fig. 5.1). Harder wood formations will resist burning longer than softer areas. When the form has been completed, the flame of a propane torch or bunsen burner can be glanced over the surface until red-hot, glowing lines appear under the flame *but not enough so that the wood continues to burn when the flame is removed.* Then, charred areas can be wiped away with a damp cloth or wire-brushed away.

The result will show a contrast of darks and lights with a predominant grain figure patterning the surface. Only simple contours lend themselves to this kind of surface treatment because the pattern of the grain can be very busy in this treatment. If the surface has many details, grain pattern and detail may "fight" one another for attention, causing an unattractive effect.

Sandblasting is another way to establish a dominant grain pattern. The end result looks very much like heating the surface except the black, or contrast of color, is not present. A detailed discussion of sandblasting is not included here, as it is an advanced technique.

Heating a metal object, such as a steel or brass form, until it is red-hot and then, in branding-iron fashion, pressing it into the wood until it burns its pattern into the surface is another texturing method using heat. Iron or brass shapes with sharply defined edges that can be attached to a dowel—which acts as a handle—are good branding tools. Look around for "found" objects. Any heat source—propane torch, candle flame, stove flame, hot plate—can be used to heat the metal brand. The steps involved in this technique are illustrated for the texturing of a box in the following series Figure 5.2a through e.

Fig. 5.2a The metal tip of a tool, in this case a nail inserted into a dowel, is heated in the flame of a propane torch.

Fig. 5.2b Then the hot tool is placed immediately onto the wood surface, burning a pattern into the wood.

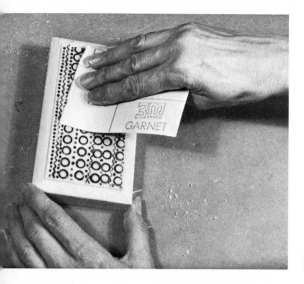

Fig. 5.2c After the design has been applied, the surface is sanded with open-coat garnet paper.

Fig. 5.2d Sawdust is brushed away and any remaining dust is removed by wiping the surface with a Tack-Cloth before applying a finish.

Fig. 5.2e The completed box, 5½ inches high and 4 inches wide.

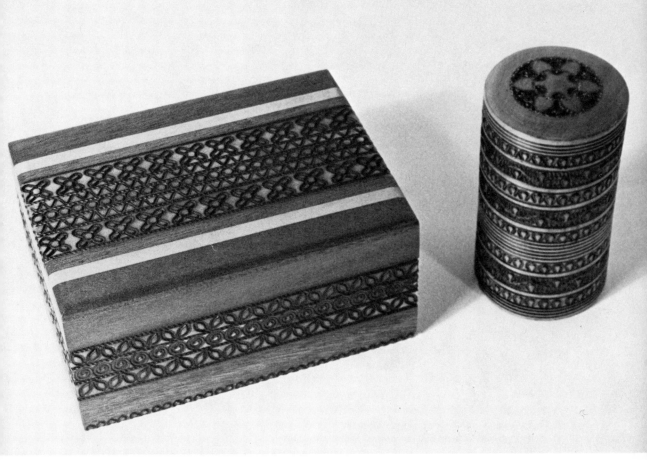

Fig. 5.3 Two boxes from Poland sport burned-in designs.

When applying the design, organize the elements into repeat patterns. Stripes, checkerboard patterns, diagonal lines, or radiating lines that result in a circle effect, are some ways to repeat elements. Several interesting patterns are shown in Figures 5.3 through 5.6.

After working with heat, perhaps the best finish for wood is to saturate it with linseed oil or several coats of varnish.

CARVING

Basic Principles Some of the basic principles of carving involve safety rules; others relate to the actual process of carving.

First, the preliminary cuts should be made to sever the grain, then the next cuts are made to chop out the chips with the tool pointed toward the first cut. The first cut, *stop cut,* then, is accomplished by pointing the tool downward, with the grain, and the second cut is then made obliquely toward that cut, as shown in Figure 5.7.

Second, always clamp the piece of wood firmly to a bench or table while you are working.

Third, do not undercut any part of a low relief carving, that is, cut under an area that is part of the design.

Fig. 5.4 The interior of the box on the left displays mitered joints, reinforced with feathers (triangular strips of wood).

Fig. 5.5 A heat-decorated box from Bulgaria, 6 inches square. Elements of the design were painted with bright enamel colors; also shown in the color section, Figure 5.

Fig. 5.6 A cutting board detailed with shallow carving and burned-in accents. By Priscilla Gagnon.

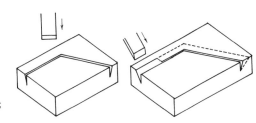

Fig. 5.7 Basic carving cuts: *left,* first cut or stop cut; *right,* cutting away.

Fourth, keep your tools clean and as sharp as razors. When tools are not used, they can be protected by being lightly oiled to minimize rusting and wrapped in flannel or soft cloth. Keep them in a dry place.

Fifth, always consider the direction of the grain; try cutting with the grain instead of fighting the wood and cutting against the grain. Of course, some cuts probably will have to be made across the grain, but this kind of cut requires very sharp tools and is much more difficult because you are actually compressing the grain.

Sixth, start from the larger concept of the shape and gradually work to details. Do not complete one section and then go on to the next. All the blocking out should be done at once, before refining the entire form.

Seventh, always wear goggles.

Eighth, always keep your hands behind the tool to avoid accidental stabbing or slicing of a hand if the tool should slip.

How to Begin Carving Select your wood block. If only smaller pieces of wood are available, you may wish to glue them together to create a thicker block. Try various arrangements before gluing anything: reverse the direction of the grain with each piece, or stack pieces in parallel formation to achieve another effect. Detailed information on lamination and appropriate glues is given in Chapter 6.

After you have chosen your block of wood or created a laminated block, study the grain pattern carefully and use a pencil to mark off the general areas to be cut away. Then the block should be firmly mounted. If you are working on a relatively small piece, a jig to work against will be sufficient, or a block may be firmly clamped to your workbench. For very large pieces, stands especially built for wood carving are equipped with a heavy duty screw that screws into the underside of the block, holding it firmly in place. However, clamps and vises can also be used—the choice of mounting devices must be practical for the size of the wood block, but is also a matter of personal preference.

Now again study the wood and its grain direction, then plan your cutting strategy. Where will you begin? In what direction will the first cut be made? Aim for a cut about an inch more shallow than the one that will eventually be required. Block out areas by chopping away the larger chunks. In the roughing out phase, be careful not to drive the gouge too deeply into the wood. Start with the larger-sized tools and, as roughing out becomes more and more fine in detail, change the size of your cutting tools to smaller ones.

Proceed slowly and carefully. Sometimes it is possible to glue a chunk of wood back into place, but it is a nuisance that takes a great deal of time. As the piece becomes more refined, chips will be smaller as well. When you have reached the point where even the smaller carving tools remove too much of the surface, switch to abrading tools, such as Surform tools, rasps, files or

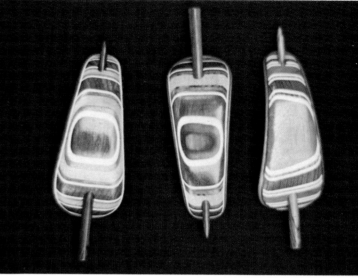

Fig. 1 *Left.* A three-dimensional puzzle sculpture by William Accorsi, about 5 inches high.

Fig. 2 *Above.* Laminated wood veneer barrettes, designed and executed by Edwin Spencer.

Fig. 3 *Below.* A storage unit of Siamese padouk, an East Indian rosewood. This project by Dennis K. Meyer is about 18 inches wide. *Courtesy: Dennis K. Meyer*

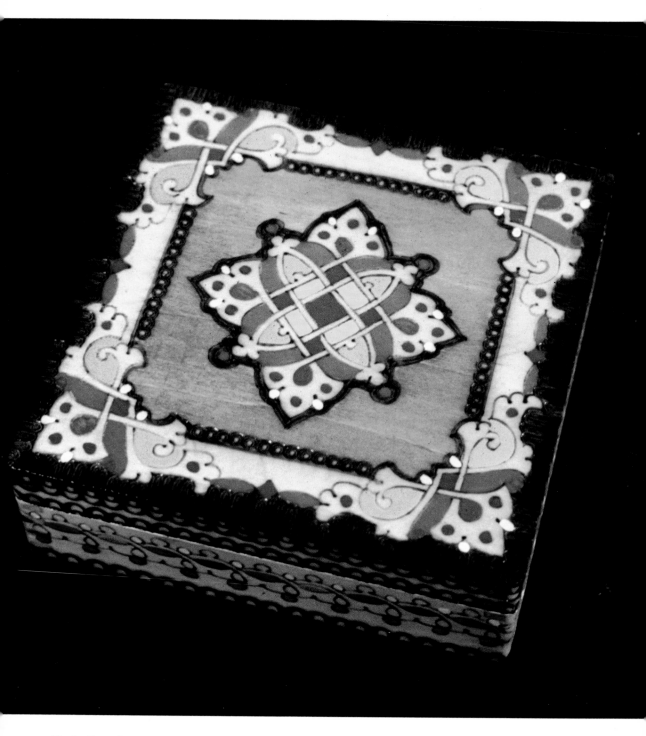

Fig. 5 *Above.* Bulgarian box, 6 inches square, decorated with a hot iron that burned in the design, then painted with colorful enamel.

Fig. 4 *Left.* Hot-water-bent veneer sculpture by Bob Ciscell. *Courtesy: Bob Ciscell*

Fig. 6   *Left.* "Wishbone," a chair by Espene

Fig. 7   *Below, left.* Priscilla Gagnon's carve
jewelry box of mahogany, walnut, and maple
Called "Frog Haven," it is 9 inches high and
inches long.

Fig. 8   *Below.* Faceplate trays by Laurence
Hendricks. *Courtesy: Laurence Hendricks*

9   *Right*. Laminated veneer, sander-shaped
klace by Edwin Spencer.

10   *Below*. Jigsaw picture puzzle with painted
ments, by the author.

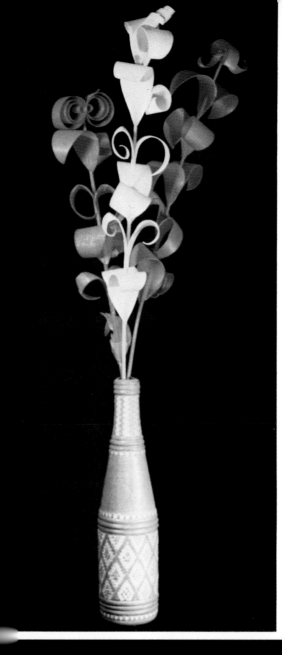

Fig. 11 *Left.* Pine veneer flowers from Scandinavia, standing about 24 inches high.

Fig. 12 *Below.* Stackable liquor storage unit by Irving Fischman. *Courtesy: Laurence 'Hendricks*

Fig. 13 *Bottom.* A box from Hungary, shallow carved with sliding lids, about 12 inches long.

Fig. 14   Hardwood vase forms, made by spindle turning.

Fig. 15   Carved and flame-textured tray from Japan.

Fig. 16   *Overleaf.* Bubinga and ebony woods are combined in this stool by Laurence Hendricks. *Courtesy: Laurence Hendricks*

sandpaper, and continue to refine the surface until you have achieved the detail and texture that you wish.

Low Relief Carving *Low relief carving,* with its variations of treatment called *incise carving, scratch carving,* or *chasing,* is cutting incisions or grooves into the surface of the wood. Most often the background and the form that is outlined remain on almost the same level. But sometimes, in low relief carving, there is an attempt at shallow modeling of the form and the background is cut away. In low relief, however, the modeling is not so pronounced as in the bas relief. Grooves with a "u" or "v" cross section are the most common incisions. These are made with a gouge, fluter, veiner, or parting tool—the cutting edges of these tools are shown in cross section in Figure 5.8.

Sugar pine has a good surface for low relief carving, and is a particularly easy-to-work wood for the beginner. Sugar pine is a white pine that does not "fight" the cutting tool. Since the fibers of the wood cling together, it is possible to get a clean, even cut across the grain. Sugar pine also has a straight grain and an even, cellular structure. One can observe, in cutting sugar pine, that it is lacking hard and soft streaks which can affect the cutting operation; yet it has some figure which can be utilized when planning the design.

To begin, make a sketch of what you want to carve. Then, when satisfied with the design, trace it onto the wood surface with pencil or stylus and carbon paper. Next, using a veiner, follow the outline, incising out narrow widths of wood. If your tool tears the wood fibers, then you probably are cutting against the grain and your tool requires sharpening.

After incising the outline, if the background is to be lowered, then use a wide gouge to roughly cut out the area. Wherever possible, work across the grain to the stop cut, which is your original incised outline. Be careful not to undercut (going under your design with the tool). Sometimes this happens by accident when too much pressure is placed on the tool. You might want to set up another line of vertical stop cuts about ¼ inch from the design so this does not happen. Later you can cut this protecting strip of wood away. The degree of tool marking that you want to keep is up to you. It may be pleasing and help the design if you allow some tool texturing to remain.

Bosting or rough carving of the raised design, or the design to be modeled, is the roughing out of parts of the design. In this operation, cutting does not go to the final depth. This is saved for the final shaping or modeling of the form. At the modeling stage, cuts more closely follow contours. For instance, a flower petal may have a curved central portion; in this case, one controlled precise cut with a narrow gouge will accomplish the task rather than, as in bosting, cutting many small chips. The photographic series in Figure 5.9 shows the steps in carving a plaque.

It is a good idea to have a lamp near

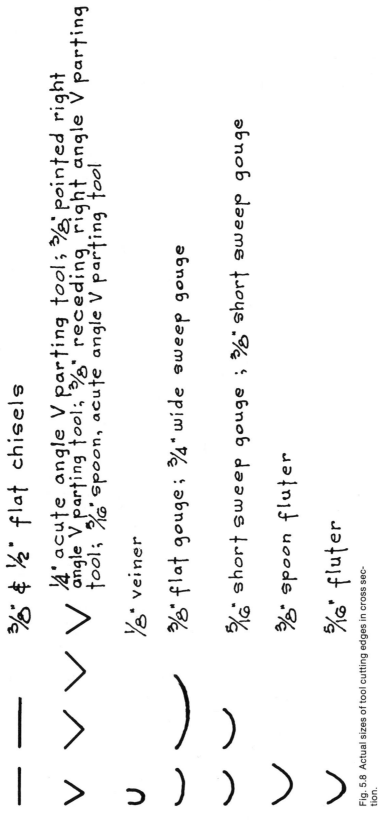

⅜" & ½" flat chisels

¼" acute angle V parting tool; ⅜" pointed right angle V parting tool; ⅜" receding right angle V parting tool; ⅜" spoon, acute angle V parting tool

⅛" veiner

⅜" flat gouge; ¾" wide sweep gouge

5/16" short sweep gouge; ⅜" short sweep gouge

⅜" spoon fluter

5/16" fluter

Fig. 5.8 Actual sizes of tool cutting edges in cross section.

Fig. 5.9a Making an inlayed and carved wooden plaque in Taiwan. First strokes are the stop cuts, accomplished by hitting the top of a chisel with a piece of hardwood or a mallet.

Fig. 5.9b The second stroke is carving toward the stop cut.

Fig. 5.9c A piece of different colored wood is to be inlayed onto the plaque. Here the pattern is being outlined on a wood scrap.

Fig. 5.9d A piece to be inlayed is trimmed to accurate dimensions with a knife. All pieces to be inlayed are glued to the background.

Fig. 5.9e Some parts are carved out of the background, others are added by carving and gluing them. The carvings are by Cheng Yu-Lin of Taipei, Taiwan.

your work so you can judge the play of light and shadow. It is, after all, light that finally models the form. A play of light over your carving will tell you whether a detail is too coarse, too shallow, or even too deep. Figures 5.10 through 5.12 show some unique examples of shallow carving.

Chip Carving *Chip carving* is another variation of low relief carving. It is the process of cutting triangular, wedge-shaped chips from the wood. The deepest part of the chip is at the apex of the triangle, and the most shallow portion is at the base, which is usually nearest to the surface; the basic strokes are illus-

trated in Figure 5.13. It is amazing how many variations can be achieved just using various shapes of triangles as the common denominator. The most important aspect of chip carving is that the edges must be sharp and crisp.

Perhaps the best way to begin chip carving is to use knives. The sharp knife blade is used to stick or strike into the wood, and the second stroke is to split or slice the wood and chip out the piece. After some experience with knives, which are easier to control, a skew chisel and "v" parting tools can be used. Some fine examples of chip carving are shown in Figures 5.14 through 5.17.

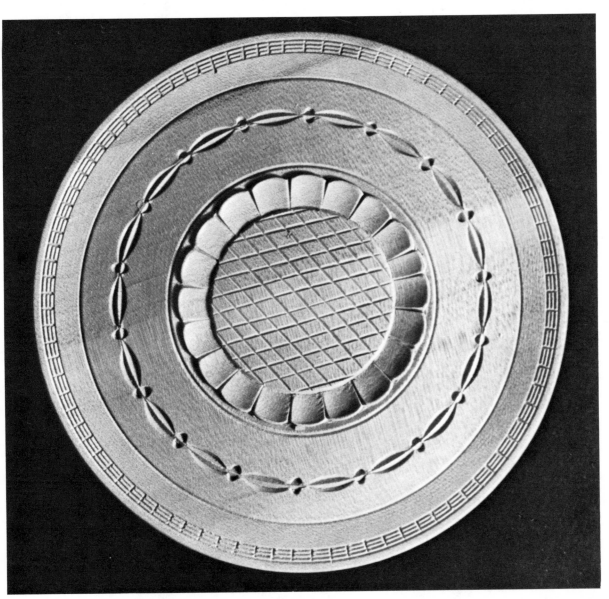

Fig. 5.10 A shallow carved, decorative plate from
Bulgaria, 9 inches in diameter.

Fig. 5.11 A shallow carved box from Thailand, 5½ inches wide by 4½ inches high.

Fig. 5.12 The lids of this Hungarian box slide into grooves. Their surfaces are incised and carved in shallow relief. This box, with three interior compartments, is shown in color, Figure 13.

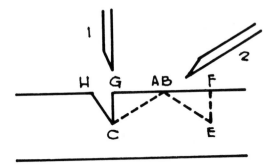
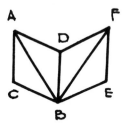

Fig. 5.13 Chip carving strokes. The first stroke (*left*) with a chisel or knife is pressed downward from *G* to *C* to the deepest part of the cut to form a stop cut; or, from *F* to *E* to cut a side and also act as a stop cut. The second stroke in a basic chip carving cut is on the diagonal: from *AB* to *C*, or *H* to *C*, or *AB* to *E*.

High Relief or Bas Relief Carving

After carving successfully in low relief, a logical progression would be toward high relief or bas relief, which takes more skill. Bas relief stops just short of becoming carving in-the-round or sculpture, because forms are attached to a background and are only partially in relief. But a great deal of modeling is necessary even though one does not look at all sides of the form. The end result is as if a sculpture were sliced off at some point and the flat side of the figure adhered to a background. There may also be an element of undercutting, inasmuch as parts may be in-the-round as in sculpture, projecting out from the background, e.g., a leg, arm, leaf. The amount of relief, therefore, can vary greatly; much depends upon the design. What distinguishes a shallow bas relief from low relief is that forms project away from the background much more than in a low relief design.

Most bas relief panels are carved employing an assortment of chisels that are powered by hand-administered mallet blows. A thick block of wood is clamped to a surface—unless the piece is big enough and heavy enough to resist moving when attacked by the force of a blow. Then carving proceeds.

Start the same way as for low relief carving. Incise your stop cuts and then rough out the background. By cutting away background, you automatically set your figures or forms in relief. Flat chisels and gouges are used for this procedure. Clean out corners with the fluter.

After the background has been cut

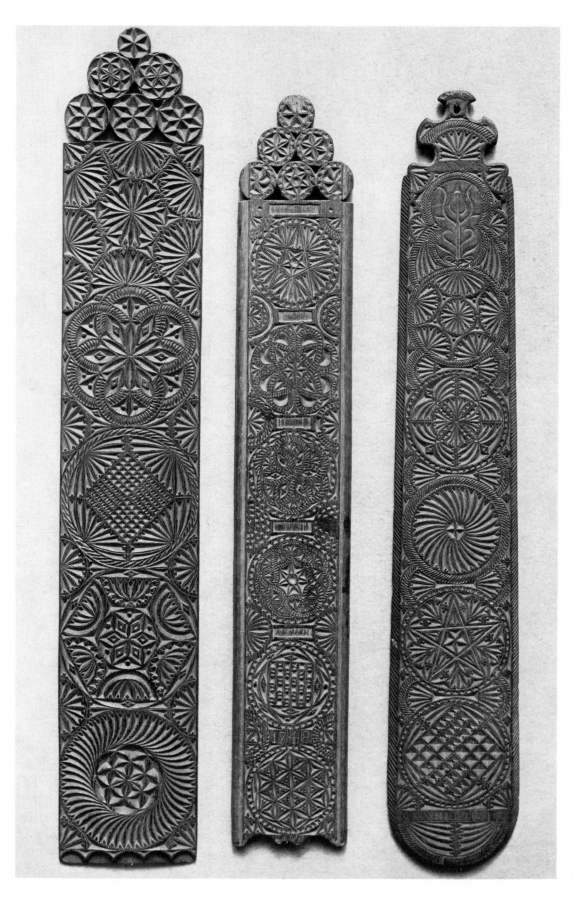

Fig. 5.14 Eighteenth-century Dutch mangle boards with chip carved designs. One is dated 1748. *Courtesy: The Metropolitan Museum of Art, Rogers Fund, 1911*

Fig. 5.15 A hot plate with chip carving and incise carving; from Surinam, South America.

Fig. 5.16 A chip carved and incised line box, with cut
areas painted white. From Yugoslavia, 10 inches long.

Fig. 5.17 A peasant's wooden spoon, 8 inches long,
with chip carved design. From Romania.

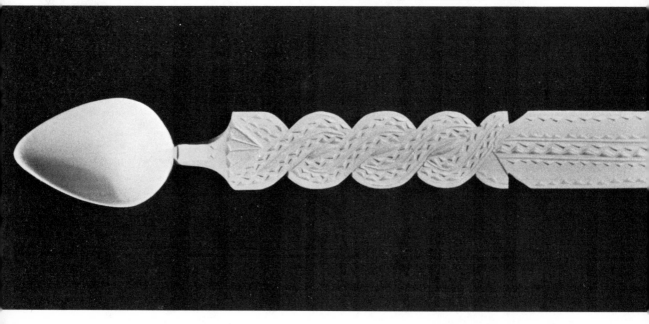

Fig. 5.18 High relief carving in the Ohrid Debar style (Yugoslavian) has a long tradition, stemming from an Old Slavian tribe that came from the Carpathian Mountains. This carving dates back to the twelfth or thirteenth century.

away, almost to the final depth, study the form that is now in relief. Think in terms of front or highest elevation, and depth or that which is further back. See the form now in planes—broad, flat expanses, frontal planes, side planes—then model your relief form aiming to achieve planes and elevations. After these directional cuts have been made, finer modeling is possible because you

Fig. 5.19 A contemporary high relief carving by Priscilla Gagnon. Several different kinds of wood have been overlayed.

have now established what will protrude most and what will appear to be more recessed.

As in low relief carving, the size of the tool will be determined, in part, by what stage you are at in modeling. Fine details are achieved with smaller gouged or finer tools. Examples of high relief are shown in Figures 5.18 and 5.19.

Objects That Can Be Carved Boxes, trivets, trays, frames, panels, doors, letter openers, bookends, furniture details, lamp bases, plates, bowls, chests, and spoon handles are just some of the possibilities that lend themselves to wood carving. In any case, carving should not be employed unless the carving is a definite improvement. Carving should not be used to mask design failure because it can't, nor should carvings be less than an integral part of the form.

LAMINATION AND THREE-DIMENSIONAL CARVING

Extending skill to three dimensions takes more expertise with carving tools, but essentially the procedures are much the same as for carving a bas relief, for instance. Implements such as wooden spoons, stirrers, bowls, cutting boards, and other useful forms can be carved directly from a block of wood. Most often the wood has to be laminated in order to build a block large enough to make a generous-sized form, although you can purchase blocks ready to carve (Fig. 6.1).

LAMINATING

Wood can be glued very easily. Usually, the lighter the wood, the more easily it can be glued. Today's glues are so strong that a piece under strain is apt to break at another point rather than the glued joint. Any of the surfaces of a piece of wood can be glued together—faces, edges, ends, or alternating all three. Patterns can be created by changing the direction of placement of the

Fig. 6.1 Blocks of wood can be laminated to obtain whatever size is desired, or they can be purchased ready-to-carve, as these solid wood cubes and cylinders (*see* Sources of Supply). *Courtesy: Gerald Jolin*

wood pieces before gluing (Figs. 6.2 and 6.3).

About Glues and Gluing The choice of glue depends upon what the piece is to be used for—for instance, is it to be used in a dry interior or will the piece be used under damp or moist conditions. Does it need to be washed or will it be exposed to weather? If the wood will be exposed to moisture, then a waterproof glue is necessary.

Wood shrinks and swells with changes in moisture content. The changes are appreciable across the grain, which swells almost twice as much as along the grain in vertical-grain stock. Therefore, the stresses on the glued joint between two flat-grain pieces of wood glued together with the grain at right angles (cross laminated) will be very large with appreciable changes in moisture content. The stresses are cut almost in half if the pieces are vertical grain; if the grain in the two pieces is parallel (laminated construction), the stresses are generally insignificant in comparison to cross-laminated construction. Also remember that different species of wood will swell and shrink at greater or lesser rates (*see* Ch. 1, Table F). The temperature at which a glue sets is also important. Directions on the product container should be followed precisely.

Today's glues actually have been developed since the 1930s. These resin glues, of various types, are products of the chemical industry and originate from such raw materials as coal, air, petro-

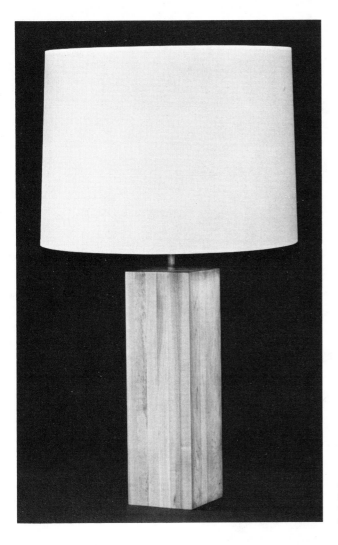

Fig. 6.2 Maple laminated together is called butcher block. Here is an example in a lamp 36 inches high, by George Kovacs Lighting Inc. *Courtesy: George Kovacs Lighting Inc.*

leum or natural gas, and water. Most of the resin glues, except the polyvinyl emulsion glues (Sobo, Elmer's, etc.) are thermosetting types. This means that once the glue has cured, or set, it will always maintain its consistency and will not be affected by heat, for instance. They are infusible and insoluble, once cured. The *thermoplastic glues,* such as the polyvinyls, remain in a reversible state and will soften again on heating.

Most of the *thermosetting resin glues,* such as urea-formaldehyde and phenol-formaldehyde, include formaldehyde as a major ingredient. Catalysts are included in or with the glue in some form. Some are sold in a single package ready

to use, or as a powder to mix with water. Others require the mixing of catalysts.

There are also *phenol resin glues* that require hot pressing at 260°F. These are used essentially in plywood construction and are not suitable for small-scale or hobby work.

The *resorcinol and phenol-resorcinol resin glues* are generally supplied as liquids to which a curing agent is added before use. They can be cured at room temperature (70°F.) and are good for work where moisture is a factor.

The working life of glue after it is accurately measured and mixed depends upon the kind of glue that it is. These facts are indicated on the glue con-

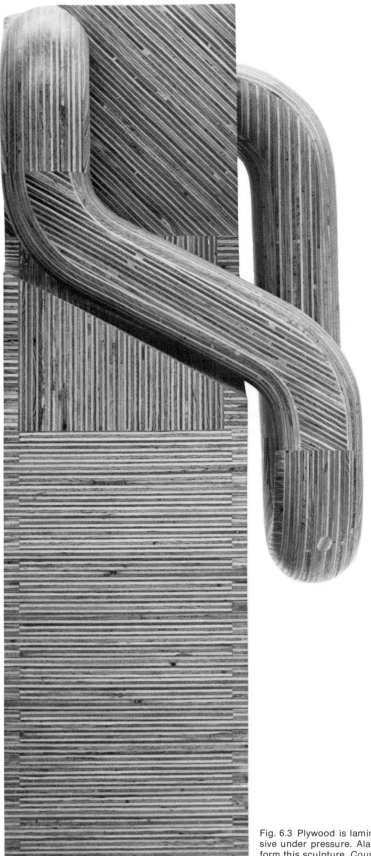

Fig. 6.3 Plywood is laminated with plastic resin adhesive under pressure. Alan Friedman used plywood to form this sculpture. *Courtesy: Alan Friedman*

tainer. In general, soon after mixing, the thermosetting resin glues begin a chemical reaction that ultimately ends in its curing and hardening. Working life of the glue, once it has been mixed, varies from a few hours to days for others. Although most of these glues harden in a few hours, they may not mature to maximum strength for several days.

Generally the wood surface should be surfaced or leveled just prior to application of the glue to avoid undesirable distortions due to any future moisture changes. The two surfaces to be joined should be smooth, clean, and flat so that they will fit uniformly when in contact with the glue. The amount of glue to be spread varies—again see instructions on the container. Gluing pressures vary also, depending upon the glue to be used. But when pressure is applied, it should be uniformly distributed over the entire joint area and should be sufficient to bring the members into close contact and to hold them, rigidly, during the setting period.

When glued areas are to be subject to stresses, then joints of various types should be fashioned. (See Ch. 3 for kinds of joints commonly used.) There is actually no limit to the size of the piece that can be built up by gluing. Actually, the thinner the wood between the joints, the stronger the joint will be. Laminated veneers are stronger than thicker pieces of wood that have been joined with glue.

Techniques As described earlier, lamination of smaller pieces of wood into large blocks can make possible pieces that would be difficult to find and would certainly be very expensive. Grain and pattern can also be controlled by laminating pieces of wood in certain directions.

Laminations may range from adhering a thin piece of veneer to a large block of wood, all the way to gluing blocks of wood, sandwiching plywood, or gluing together many layers of veneer. Plywood itself is an example of lamination.

Probably among the best glues to use for laminating wood—whether blocks or veneer—are the plastic-resin thermosetting glues, those light-brown powders that have to be mixed with water. The glue lines left by these glues are very close to the color of the woods and are nearly invisible. Waterproof marine glues are good, too. These are usually two-component resorcinol or epoxy resins. When laminating veneers, apply the least amount that will do the job. (More glue will be needed when laminating thicker pieces.) Applying glue with a paint brush is a good idea.

After gluing pieces together, clamp them to allow for even pressure. Any excess glue that oozes out can be removed later by planing or sanding.

Making a Barrette One of the most attractive ways of forming jewelry and accessories is by laminating exotic veneers, then shaping the laminated forms. Edwin Spencer's unique jewelry is made just this way, by laminating and then carving with abrasives.

To make a hair barrette, such as those shown in color, Figure 2, Mr. Spencer starts with a stack of veneers, each layer a different color, each contrasting in color and grain. He glues them in stacks in a jig so that they line up into blocks 11½ inches long, 2 inches wide, and 1 to 2 inches high. (He often stacks many of these small blocks together to make other accessories.)

Polyvinyl acetate (pva) is the type of glue Mr. Spencer uses in laminating these exotic veneers. The gluing has to be perfect; otherwise a flaw, such as an airpocket, could ruin a piece. It shows up when carving. After the pieces of veneer are glued together and have dried for 24 hours in dry weather, he levels the surface and cuts the approximate final shape on a band saw. A jig is used to keep the band saw blade from twisting as the blade cuts around curves.

Then using a jig over a table saw, Edwin Spencer chamfers (bevels) the surfaces. Excess wood is sanded away on all sides on a sanding belt and edges are modeled in this process. The piece is constantly kept in motion on the sanding belt to avoid the formation of grooves. Figure 6.4 shows the sequence of procedures.

A brush-back sanding head is also used. This is a nylon brush that is impregnated with abrasive, made by the 3M Company (*see* Sources of Supply). The flexibility of the wheel allows for all curved surfaces to be finely sanded.

After the form has been medium-grit sanded, a hole is drilled, using a bit in a drill press, for the stick (or pin) that will slide through the body of the barrette. A wider hole is drilled at one end because the stick will be tapered.

The pin is carefully fitted now by rotating the wood on a sanding belt, and trying it out for fit through the barrette holes at various stages in the process.

The barrette is now ready for fine sanding and polishing. No waxes or oils

Fig. 6.4a Edwin Spencer stacks and glues various colors and kinds of veneer in a jig.

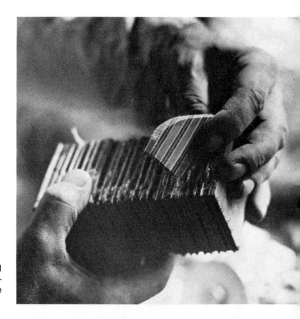

Fig. 6.4b After the glue has set, the block can be sliced in various ways. Each kind of cut yields a different pattern. The small piece held here was cut across the block so that a striped pattern resulted.

Figs. 6.4c and d When a curve is cut from top down, then shaped by sanding on various parts of belt and drum sanders, a pattern emerges.

Fig. 6.4e When the carving-by-sanding has been completed to rough contours, the barrette is buffed on a brush-backed sanding head, which is a nylon brush impregnated with abrasive. The flexibility of the wheel allows for a fine final sanding of the surface.

Fig. 6.4f Holes are drilled in the barrette and then a tapered stick is cut and then shaped on a sanding belt to fit into the two holes.

Fig. 6.4g Two completed barrettes by Edwin Spencer; also shown in color (Fig. 2).

Fig. 6.5 On the left is a roughly outlined earring form, just cut from a block. On the right is the form after shaping on power sanding devices and before a hole is made for attachment of findings.

are used. A loose (not stitched) muslin buffing wheel is used.

Occasionally, when a piece is particularly rough, a mixture of carnauba wax and diamond buffing compound is used. The piece is buffed until a high luster is achieved.

Making Earrings Edwin Spencer uses a unique system of stacking pieces of veneer to create geometric earring designs; examples in rough and finished form are shown in Figure 6.5.

Using various jigs to cut accurate angles, such as 30° and 45° angles, he then attaches these small pieces in a repeating sequence on a piece of adhesive tape. If the angles are correct, they can then be rolled up into a tube, while still on the tape, after they have been glued with a concentrated pva. In the sequence shown in Figure 6.6, a dowel is used in the center during the rolling process to adjust the position of the pieces. The rolls are allowed to dry for at least 24 hours.

Fig. 6.6a Strips of wood and laminated wood cut at precise angles are stuck side-by-side onto adhesive tape, then pulled into a circle to test matching of surfaces.

Fig. 6.6b Areas that meet are glued with white glue and wrapped around a dowel to keep alignment true. The dowel is withdrawn carefully and the piece is left to dry.

Fig. 6.6c Various combinations of patterns are possible using this technique. The adhesive tape has been removed and the cylinders are then sliced into earring disks. Edges are chamfered and the whole piece is sanded and polished as in making the barrette.

Slices are then cut off the tubelike form on a band saw or table saw. Then they are chamfered, sanded, and polished the same way as a barrette.

Figures 6.7 through 6.11 show a number of examples of unique jewelry, each item made from veneers laminated into a block or shape, then sliced, shaped, and finished.

WHITTLING OR HAND CARVING

Whittling is the cutting away of small chips or pieces of wood from a larger piece of wood by means of a knife. In fact, the term *whittling* got its name from a kind of clasp or sheath knife called a whittle that was used, among other things, for whittling. This method of

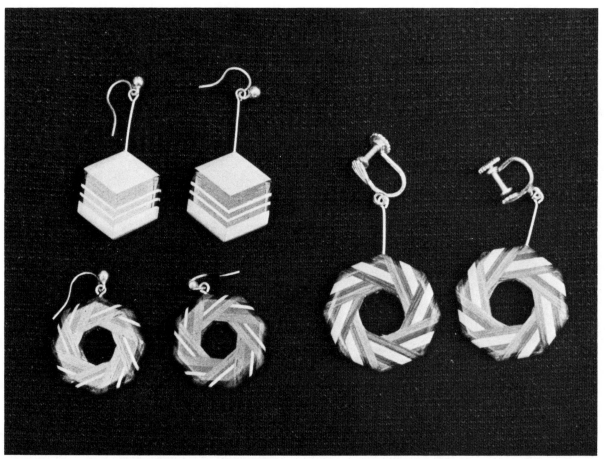

Fig. 6.7 Some earrings by Edwin Spencer.

woodcarving is thought of as a portable, leisure-time activity and brings to mind an old man, sitting in a chair in front of the general store, whittling his wooden forms. Some interesting examples of this age-old craft are shown in Figures 6.12 through 6.18.

Actually, the portability of the wood and knife or tool makes whittling a very desirable carving technique. The woods most often used are soft, nonresinous types such as sugar pine, basswood, poplar, cottonwood, and cedar, although many kinds are suitable.

When whittling, your hands serve as clamps and a sharp knife or carving tool cuts away the surfaces. If you are right handed, the left hand is used to hold the work firmly; the right hand holds the carving tool while part of the hand rests

Fig. 6.8 Another variation on lamination in jewelry making illustrated in this necklace by Edwin Spencer.

on the work. To do this, grip the tool as close to the edge of the blade as possible. It may be necessary at times to carve away from your body, particularly when excising larger areas, or to carve in toward the body, with the thumb used to support the wood. Finer details are done this way. Or you may incise cuts with the point of the blade, to achieve delicate details.

To begin, sketch the rough contours of the form on all sides of a block of wood after studying the grain. Then cut away the rough dimensions. You can do this with a band saw, a Dremel Moto-Saw, or a coping saw, if the piece is small. When the wood has been roughly cut into contours, proceed to rough out top, bottom, back, front, sides—in fact, all around the shape—with gouges. Then

Fig. 6.9 Two pendant necklaces by Edwin Spencer made the same way as the barrette.

Fig. 6.10 A bracelet strung on elastic, by Edwin Spencer.

Fig. 6.11 Some rings that also utilize the same technique. By Edwin Spencer.

continue to cut away small pieces until the form is completely refined.

Finishing of the surface is the last step. Varnishing or oiling are the most preferable finishes because they serve to seal the pores while at the same time allowing the quality and color of the wood to show through without much alteration of color or texture.

Whittling is a fine introduction to a more difficult kind of carving—direct carving of large forms.

DIRECT CARVING

Direct carving involves the subtraction of wood from a whole by means of cutting and/or abrading tools (see Ch. 5). When beginning an ambitious piece,

it is best to make a small, three-dimensional model of the piece in clay, soap, papier mâché, plaster of Paris, or whatever forming material is available. This model can be modified and, when approved, can be enlarged into the wooden form. Proportions can then be transposed by approximating the translation of size by eye or with calipers. Measurements can be counted using graph paper—such as 1 inch to the foot (one square equals twelve squares) or whatever proportional enlargements are desired.

As in any kind of carving, sharp tools are a necessity. And if the piece is large, it should be mounted by means of a bench screw or various kinds of vises or clamps onto a steady surface. Mounting and carving methods are illustrated

Fig. 6.12 A Bantu man from Tanzania, East Africa, whittling a wooden sculpture using a penknife. Note how he controls the knife with his thumb. *Taken from* Contemporary African Arts and Crafts *by Thelma R. Newman. © 1974 by Thelma R. Newman. Used by permission of Crown Publishers, Inc.*

Fig. 6.13 Small wooden sculpture carved by whittling. By Senafu people, Ivory Coast, West Africa. *Taken from* Contemporary African Arts and Crafts *by Thelma R. Newman. © 1974 by Thelma R. Newman. Used by permission of Crown Publishers, Inc.*

in Figure 6.19. Procedures are the same as for making a bas relief. The first cuts are large, general ones, blocking out the form. If the piece has been laminated of several pieces of wood, the wood can be cut before lamination into the general proportions (and glued that way) to minimize wasteful cutting away of unwanted areas. As cutting proceeds, the work becomes closer and closer to the refined

Fig. 6.14a Whittling can be done on site with small pieces of wood. The pieces shown here are wood thorns of various colors that grow in Nigeria.

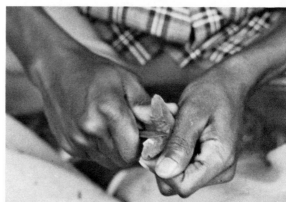

Fig. 6.14b Woodlike, these thorns can be whittled into shape with a carving knife. The arm of a man is being formed here.

Fig. 6.14c After the various small parts are carved, they are glued into place in the boat with a glue made from boiled rice and water.

Fig. 6.14d The completed carving, approximately 4 inches high, by Ola Fesese of Nigeria. *Taken from* Contemporary African Arts and Crafts *by Thelma R. Newman.* © *1974 by Thelma R. Newman. Used by permission of Crown Publishers, Inc.*

Fig. 6.15 Another thorn carving by Ola Fesese. *Taken from* Contemporary African Arts and Crafts *by Thelma R. Newman.* © *1974 by Thelma R. Newman. Used by permission of Crown Publishers, Inc.*

Fig. 6.16 Small figurines from Mexico, whittled from softwood.

Fig. 6.17 Symbolic forms whittled by the Cuna Indians, San Blas, Panama.

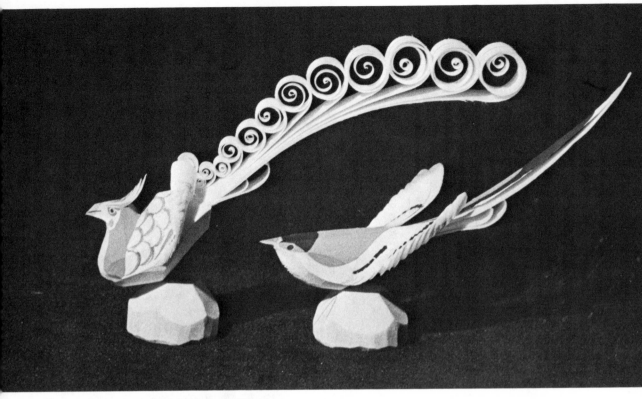

Fig. 6.18 Decorative forms from Japan, whittled from pine. Characteristic details are painted on; the remaining wood is kept in its natural state.

Fig. 6.19a When a large, heavy, unwieldy block of wood is to be carved, it is best to mount it to a carving stand. Here a bench mounting screw is being twisted into a laminated block of wood.

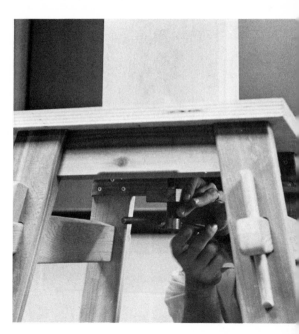

Fig. 6.19b The piece is attached to the bench for firm mounting.

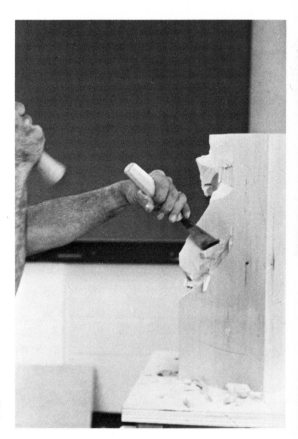

Fig. 6.19c First cuts are made to block out the form. At this point a larger chisel is being used to make a stop cut . . .

Fig. 6.19d . . . and in the second cut, the chisel is hit toward the stop cut, resulting in the removal of a chunk of wood.

Fig. 6.19e The completed sculpture.

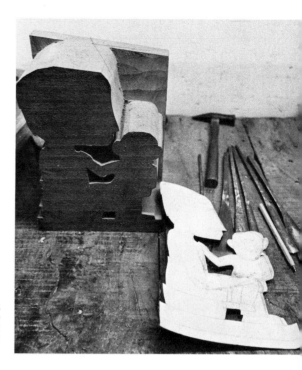

Fig. 6.20 A drawing is made indicating one view of a sculpture. This is cut out of paper and, in template fashion, traced onto a block of wood. The wood is cut to the contour and the rest of the form is modeled with various chisels and gouges. From Taipei, Taiwan.

Fig. 6.21a In Africa, as in many parts of the world, an ancient tool—the adz—is used to block out major areas of a form.

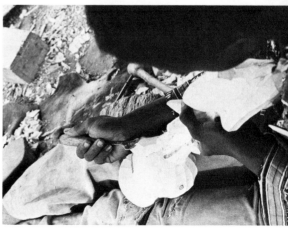

Fig. 6.21b After large areas are cut away, smaller cutting tools are used to refine the carving. The spoon-shaped knife is used to scoop out areas and carve concavities.

Fig. 6.21c Green wood is used because it is softer. The result is a magnificent sculpture that is likely to crack unless the wood surface is well protected. Even the very large piece in the foreground was not mounted for carving. Carver from northern Ivory Coast. *Taken from* Contemporary African Arts and Crafts, *by Thelma R. Newman. © 1974 Thelma R. Newman. Used by permission of Crown Publishers, Inc.*

Fig. 6.22 A jewelry box called "Frog Haven" in mahogany, walnut, and maple. By Priscilla Gagnon, the form is 9 inches high, 16 inches long, and 13½ inches across the flower. *Courtesy: Priscilla Gagnon*

Fig. 6.23 Top view of "Frog Haven," also shown in the color section, Figure 7. *Courtesy: Priscilla Gagnon*

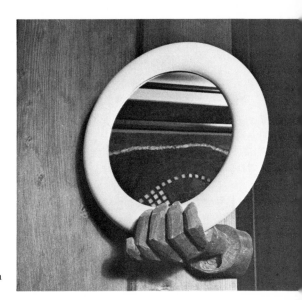

Fig. 6.24 A hand, 6 inches high, carved to hold a mirror. By Joyce and Edgar Anderson.

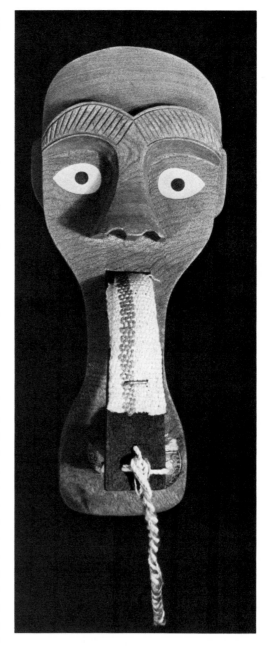

Fig. 6.25 A door knocker by Cheng Yu-Lin of Taipei, Taiwan. The knocker is 9 inches high and the eyes are inlaid.

form of the original model. Details are added last. If parts are to project, they can be carved separately and added later with a plugged and glued joint.

Another approach is to enlarge a sketch onto graph paper and then cut out patterns for all sides, then trace them onto the corresponding sides of the block of wood (Fig. 6.20). Of course, as with any carving operation, one of the first considerations in planning a design for wood is to consider the pattern formed by the grain and to try to design for that particular grain, taking advantage of natural curves and working with them in carving so that they function as part of the piece.

Some people have difficulty carving forms from a solid. It certainly is easier to build up forms from bits and pieces than to visualize a subtracted form from a whole. That is why making a three-dimensional sketch from a material such as clay is advisable, so that the experience of seeing a whole has been achieved before the more difficult chipping away process begins. An intermediate step of drawing and tracing patterns of the sides onto a piece of wood also helps the visualization process. Try to limit the amount of wood that is to be cut away at any one time. If you have trepidations, proceed to chip away small bits at a time, else you may start out making an elephant and end up with an ant.

Fig. 6.26 Carved mirror, richly textured, by Louise Odes-Neaderland. *Courtesy: Louise Odes-Neaderland*

The photographic series in Figure 6.21 shows an artist carving with the use of an ancient tool, the adz. A variety of carved forms, both functional and decorative, created by various artists are shown in Figures 6.22 through 6.31.

Carving with Power Tools Power carving tools can speed up the roughing out and detailing processes of carving wood. However, speed can ruin a piece, so the best advice is to go slowly.

Flexible shaft tools, equipped with speed controls, and hand-held drills fitted with various Surform barrel-shaped cutting tools, are safe and easy to use (Fig. 6.32). Drill bits, grinding wheels, sanding drums and disks, disk

Fig. 6.27 Two pendants by Joyce Anderson. Nature's insects carved the surface texture.

Fig. 6.28 Carved rings by Joyce Anderson: one is highly textured, the others as smooth as glass.

Fig. 6.29 African mahogany bowl, 16 inches long. The bowl was carved completely from a single block with Surform tools. By the author.

Fig. 6.30 A carved walnut bowl from Thailand; 11 inches in diameter, 5¼ inches high.

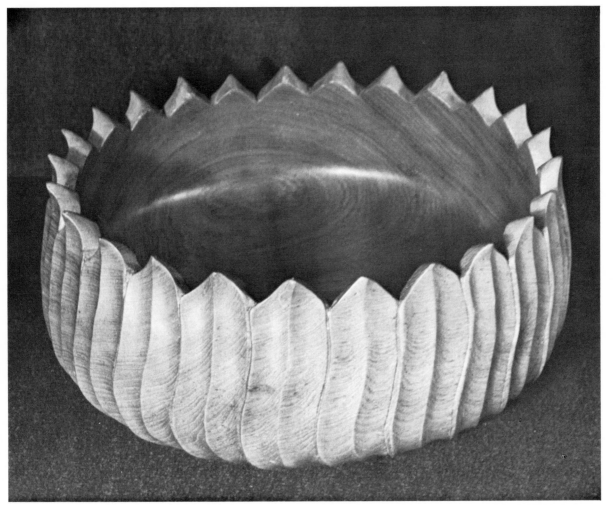

Fig. 6.31 "Pony Tail," a sculpture 42 inches high in black walnut by David Hostetler.

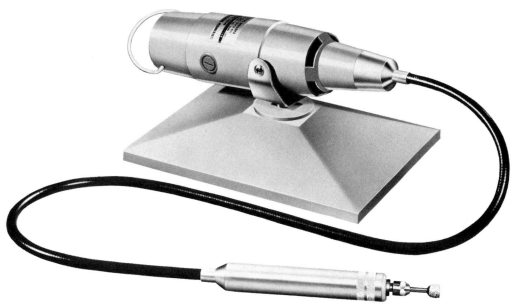

Fig. 6.32 One type of power carving is possible through use of various abrading bits attached to drills. Dremel's Flexible Shaft Moto-Tool #232 is one such tool that is easy to wield. When hooked into a foot-controlled rheostat, various speeds can be obtained. *Courtesy: Dremel Corp.*

saws and abrasive cutoff wheels can function here as well.

To maintain control, make several light cuts rather than exert pressure and speed to cut away one large chunk. If the bit starts to turn blue and the wood begins to smoke, you are using too high a speed or exerting too much pressure for that particular tool. *Always wear* *safety glasses or goggles and a face* *shield when working with power tools.* And always follow the instructions accompanying the tools. Remember that the power of the tool, spinning at 20,000 rpm, can propel enough force on a chip of wood to do a great deal of damage to you.

TURNING WOOD ON A LATHE

Wood turning is a basic woodworking technique that combines the skill of hand tool work with the power of a machine. Once, when there was no electric or gas motor-driven machine power, human energy was used to turn wood with such devices as twisted cord, a foot treadle, water power, etc. Occasionally one can still find hobbyists working this way. Essentially, the process is the same whether the wood is turned by hand or machine. The mechanism that holds the wood while it is being turned is a *lathe*. A lathe is a machine to which a piece of wood can be fixed and then revolved. Shapes are carved into the revolving wood with tools.

WOOD-TURNING EQUIPMENT

Lathes: Types and Capabilities Small lathes can be built using variable speed drills fitted with attachments to convert them to wood-turning machines. There is also a small lathe manufactured by

Fig. 7.1 Dremel Moto-Lathe: perfect for small work, such as nut bowls, candlesticks, and lamp bases.

Dremel that is a good machine to introduce the woodworker to the process of turning (Fig. 7.1). Both the drill conversion technique and the Dremel lathe are fine for making small items such as egg cups, nut bowls, candlesticks, lamp bases, and small parts for miniature work.

For those who wish to expand to bigger forms, a lathe powered by a motor of at least ½ hp is capable of turning a wood disk for a bowl 4 inches deep and 12 inches in diameter, and turning a spindle 4 inches in diameter and 2 feet, 6 inches long between centers (Fig. 7.2). Lathe size is indicated by the largest diameter that can be turned, by the bed length, and by the distance between centers—the overall length.

A lathe may be belt driven, using step pulleys, or it may have a variable speed pulley or a direct-drive motor. It is necessary to be able to adjust the speed of the lathe for different sizes of items being turned (Table I). Generally, the larger the form to be turned, the lower the speed.

The selection of wood for turning is also critical (Table J). Some woods, like beech and pecan, turn relatively well regardless of moisture content. Other woods, like cottonwood and willow, give good turnings only if dried down to about 6 percent moisture content. Generally, heavier woods turn better than lightweight ones; and heavy pieces turn better than light pieces of the same type of wood.

Wood-Turning Tools The tools used for cutting and turning wood into shapes are generally six types: *gouges* for roughing stock to round shapes; *skews*

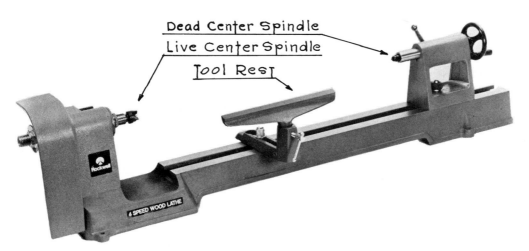

Fig. 7.2 Wood-turning lathe. *Courtesy: Rockwell International*

for smooth cutting to finish a surface; *parting tools* to cut recesses and separate pieces; *spear-pointed* or *diamond tools* to finish inside surfaces, recesses, or curved corners; *flat tools* to scrape straight surfaces; and *round-nose tools* for scraping concavities, recesses, and circular grooves. Also necessary and good to have on hand are rulers, dividers, and inside and outside calipers.

This array of tools (Fig. 7.3) accomplishes two basic kinds of opera-tions—cutting and scraping. Gouges, skews, and parting tools cut; flat-nose, round-nose, and spear-pointed tools scrape. But cutting tools can also be used for scraping operations. In cutting, the outer skin of the wood is pierced and the wood is then peeled off as a shaving. In scraping, the tool scrapes away small bits of wood particles. These tools are utilized with the lathe in two kinds of turning: *spindle turning,* or turning between centers, and *faceplate turning,* or turning at the end of the lathe.

Table I. Suggested Lathe Speeds

SIZE	ROUGHING (RPM)	GENERAL (RPM)	FINISHING (RPM)
under 2″	900–1300	2400–2800	3000–4000
2″–4″	600–1000	1800–2400	2400–3000
4″–6″	600–800	1200–1800	1800–2400
6″–8″	400–600	800–1200	1200–1800
8″–10″	300–400	600–800	1200–1800
over 10″	300	300–600	600–900

Table J. Relative Yield of Smooth Turnings in Percentages

Beech	93	Oak, red	84	Maple, soft	78
Pecan	89	Oak, white	82	Gum, black	75
Gum, red and sap	86	Ash	81	Elm, soft	70
Hickory	86	Hackberry	79	Basswood	70
Sycamore	85	Magnolia	79	Cottonwood	70
Poplar, yellow	84	Tupelo	79	Willow	60

From Donald G. Coleman, "Properties, Selection, and Suitability of Woods for Woodworking," Forest Products Laboratory, Forest Service, U.S. Department of Agriculture

Fig. 7.3 An array of wood-turning tools, custom made for Peter Child. These tools vary substantially from manufacturer to manufacturer, from country to country.

Cutting tools must be sharp if they are to perform without digging in, clattering, and otherwise messing up a turning. Grindstones are probably the easiest sharpening devices. A dry Carborundum wheel running at about 3000 rpm without any oil stone or stropping is enough. A keen burr-edge can be achieved this way if no pressure is used against the wheel. Otherwise, the steel will burn. The stone must have a matte surface, free of shine, because with shine on the wheel more pressure is needed to sharpen the tool and this will guarantee ruining the tool.

To keep a shine from forming, a star wheel abrasive dresser run over the wheel periodically will keep the grindstone in good condition and maintain its matte, grey surface. The dressing tool will also straighten a wheel that is malformed and grooved. Dipping a tool that has just been sharpened into cold water will also insure against overheating. If an extra keen edge is desired, then a final honing on an Arkansas stone using some oil, followed by stropping on leather, will do the trick.

To grind the tool to a sharp edge (as shown in Figure 7.4), rest the tool perpendicularly against the stone on the tool rest so that the heel of the bevel is rubbing. Then roll the blade slowly from side to side. Gently and slowly lift the handle and "spread" the bevel toward the edge. As the tool is resting against the stone, the bevel slowly takes on the curvature of the wheel. This is called *hollow grinding*. Take care not to lift the gouge tool too frequently, else you will produce uneven grinding. If yours is a new tool and you find the edges going ragged, don't mind it. This happens. After use, the first edge will wear away and the resulting edges will be more even.

Figs. 7.4a and b Tool sharpening is accomplished on an intermediate dry grit stone of Carborundum, 6 inches by 1 inch, running at 3000 rpm. The safety speed of the stone is marked on its side: *never exceed this.* Do not use pressure on the stone, just hold the tool at the proper angle.

Fig. 7.4c The sharpened tool edge from a grindstone is not so good as from an oil stone, but it is adequate. To sharpen the tool to a finer edge, try stropping the edge on a piece of leather after first rotating it in a circular motion on an oil-coated oil stone. The chisel is the only tool that Peter Child, the English woodturner, hones because it is a finishing tool.

Fig. 7.4d When the stone develops a shine, clean it with a star wheel abrasive dresser as shown here.

Objects That Can Be Made by Turning
A wide range of objects can be turned. Table tops, cheese and bread boards, plates, bowls, and egg cups, to name a few, can be faceplate turned. Chair legs, egg timers, cylinder containers of all types, table lights, napkin rings, covers for containers, and decorative objects, such as wooden eggs, can be spindle turned. And of course, elements can be turned which will be used and attached to other parts made through other processes.

As with all skills, wood turning takes practice to achieve "perfection."

SPINDLE TURNING

In *spindle turning,* turning a cylinder, a length of wood is turned between a *moving* (live) center or element and a *stationary* (dead) center that is used to hold the other end of the wood. In turning a cylinder, the wood is held between the moving and stationary points, and as the piece rotates *toward* you, a gouge or other type of chisel is used to cut away the square corners until the piece becomes a cylinder. After rounding off the wood, various shapes can be cut or scraped into the cylinder.

Attaching Wood to Lathe Before attaching the wood to the lathe and beginning to turn, the centers at each end of the piece must be located by crossing two diagonal lines from corner to corner. Where the lines intersect, you have the center. The spurs belonging to the lathe are placed in the center positions at each end and are struck into the wood with a mallet until they are seated securely. It is a good idea to oil the spur at the stationary center. With spurs attached, the wood is placed between the centers on the lathe and the tool rest is adjusted so that it clears the wood by about ⅛ inch, with the top of the tool rest set at about ⅛ inch above center. Then the speed of the lathe is adjusted according to the diameter of the piece (*see* Table I). Start at the slowest speeds for that diameter first.

Cutting and Scraping When the lathe is turned on, a shadow will appear, indicating where the corners are. Put on your goggles and plant your feet firmly in front of the lathe and stand erect. The gouge should be held with the handle down, the blade on the rest; the right hand holds the handle firmly with the left hand gently and comfortably over the blade, guiding it (Fig. 7.5). The thumb is a good pivoting "tool." To begin, push the blade forward slowly until it makes contact with the corners of the revolving wood. Small chips will come flying off. Retaining that angle of contact, move the gouge back and forth along the wood until the corners have been rounded and a rough cylinder formed. It is best to look at the top of the revolving wood, not at the gouge. Aim to cut, rather than scrape, the wood.

Refinement of the cylinder can be made with a skew chisel. The skew should rest on its side, with its cutting edge aimed slightly above the cylinder.

Fig. 7.5a With his lathe running at 2000 rpm, Peter Child has just removed the square corners from a block of soft pine. The form is now a cylinder. Notice his position when holding the skew chisel.

Fig. 7.5b With a gouge, he has indicated where change of shape will be on the cylinder.

Fig. 7.5c Mr. Child now cuts away areas with a deep fluted gouge, creating indentations. Note that the tool handle is slightly lower than the blade. This is the proper cutting angle.

Fig. 7.5d He rolls the parting tool toward the right when going right, to the left when going left. The degree of roll (pivoting of the tool) depends upon the size of the form.

Fig. 7.5e Here a parting tool is used to create sharp indentations.

The upper part of the skew is called the *toe* and the lower part of the skew, the *heel*. Hold the side of the tool firmly against the tool rest, and slowly draw the skew back until the cutting edge is over the cylinder at a point about halfway between the heel and toe. Keep the handle down and the tool high enough above center so that the point of the tool does not get caught in the downward movement of the lathe and tear the tool out of your hand.

With some practice, cylinders can be tapered and variations can be made in the surface with cutting beads. A *bead and parting tool* is used in parting-tool fashion to cut notches into the cylinder. The tool is pushed into the wood. With indentations established at various points along the cylinder, areas between the notches can be rounded. Rotating the tool helps to create rounded effects. Fingers are used as a pivot, with the handle rolled round to the right, then to the left. As the cut is completed, the handle will be held higher. To finish a taper, always cut from the larger to the smaller diameter.

To use the scraping method, hold the gouge in a vertical position and keep the handle high enough so that the cutting edge is pointed at a line of the center. To begin a scraping action, hold the tool flat and force it into the wood.

To duplicate shapes and calibrate against other shapes in order to repeat them, as in the spindle designs of four chair legs, use calipers and their points

Fig. 7.6 A fine example of a spindle turned lamp base of western pine, 26 inches high. By George Kovacs Lighting Inc. *Courtesy: George Kovacs Lighting Inc.*

to slightly mark the work, transferring measurements from the model to the piece being turned.

Remember, wood-turning tools must always be kept sharp.

FACEPLATE TURNING

Usually, the products of faceplate turning are bowls and similar circular objects. In *faceplate* turning, the wood is fastened to a faceplate and shaped by tools as the wood revolves on the end of the lathe.

Preparation Generally, a faceplate is screwed onto the center of a block of wood. It is a good idea to cut the block on a band saw to a disk shape at least ¼ inch larger than the finished diameter.

If screw holes will interfere with the design of the finished object, particularly if the form is a small one, then glue a piece of wood to the wood to be turned, using brown wrapping paper between the two pieces of wood so that they will separate easily later; fasten the faceplate to the extra wood. After the faceplate has been attached and the spindle is in place on the lathe, locate the center of the piece and adjust the tool rest across the edge of the wood.

Turning the Form Set the lathe to a slow speed at the beginning. Use a flat round-nose or spear-pointed tool to dress the outside of the disk (finish or refine the surface). Then readjust the tool rest across the diameter of the wood; it will pull your tool upward.

With the wood dressed on the outside and face, the shaping begins. Use various turning tools to remove as much waste as needed and gradually refine the shape, as demonstrated by Peter Child in the sequence in Figure 7.7. The outside or the inside can be done first;

Fig. 7.7a Peter Child rough turns a bowl of green wood and puts it aside to season for 6–8 months at normal temperature away from heat, rain, sun, but where air can dry it. Air dries wood an inch per year: if he turns a bowl into one-inch walls, he leaves it to season a year. Here he prepares a piece of wood for turning. A block has been cut on a band saw into a round shape. He is using a template to indicate where holes are in the faceplate, marking them with an awl. Then they are drilled before the faceplate is screwed into place.

Fig. 7.7b This bowl was brought out of its resting place. It was warped, as was expected. With a ½-inch gouge, starting at the back and working forward, the outside is being trimmed.

Fig. 7.7c With the tool rest readjusted, the interior of the bowl is cut with a ½-inch to ¼-inch gouge, working from larger to smaller tools as the surface is refined. With the cutting gouge, he works from the center, or slightly above the center, to the outside.

Fig. 7.7d The edge is trimmed.

Fig. 7.7e The tool rest is readjusted and a scraper is used at the center or slightly below the center of the piece, held horizontally and level. The scraper is used as a finishing tool, *not* a wood removal tool.

Fig. 7.7f Here, a rounded scraper is used to trim and finish the bowl's interior, working from the outside to the center.

Fig. 7.7g The dimple or pimple is removed from the center by pulling the scraper astride the center, moving from left to right. All this is done at the low speed of 700 rpm.

Fig. 7.7h Hands are human calipers sensing the thickness of the side of the bowl, judging whether the sides are even and where additional trimming is necessary.

Fig. 7.7i Open-coat garnet paper in a finishing grade (not cabinet grade) is used, starting with #100 grit and ending with #220. The direction of the wheel is reversed at one point so one can get the same smooth effect as in hand sanding, where the direction is alternated.

Fig. 7.7j After the faceplate is removed, the base is sanded with an orbital sander. The faceplate can be seen on the right.

Fig. 7.7k The bowl is then oiled.

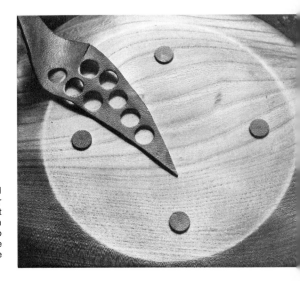

Fig. 7.7l Rounds are punched out of leather and glued over the holes left by the screws of the faceplate. Other alternatives are to use a disk of wood and adhere it with animal glue to the wood to be turned with brown paper in between prior to attaching the faceplate; or to swell up the holes with wet cotton batting, using the heat of a hot iron; or to use a wood filler to fill the holes; or to place felt over the entire base.

Fig. 7.7m The completed bowl by Peter Child.

Fig. 7.8 Another wood bowl by Peter Child.

but each time the tool rest has to be re-aligned.

Fingers are used to judge the evenness of the walls. Usually, the thickness of the rim determines what thickness the walls should be—unless the design clearly requires a tapering of some kind.

Finishing After refining through turning until the surface of the wood is quite smooth to touch, abrasives can be used to finish the wood. This is followed by oiling and waxing the piece while it is still on the wheel. Very little use of sandpaper will be necessary if turning was well done. An open-coat garnet paper is best in at least 100 grit. Anything coarser than that will leave marks in the wood. Set the lathe at slow speed when using sandpaper.

After sanding, a hard carnauba wax can be applied while the wheel is turning at slow speed. Use a soft cloth for the application of the wax. After the wax has hardened for a while, buff with a soft woolen cloth.

Another good finishing material is a mixture of one part carnauba wax mixed with three parts of beeswax by weight, with just enough refined turpentine to cover the mixture. The whole mixture is melted in a double boiler until it is liquid, like butter. Allow it to cool and apply the cold wax to the revolving wood so that friction spreads a thin layer over the wood. Use a soft dry cloth to drive the polish into the wood. Some craftsmen leave the wax on overnight, then polish or buff the piece the next day. Shavings from teak wood, which is oily, are also used. Teak oil is also used for finishing turned pieces.

When the form is removed from the faceplate, screw holes can be covered with rounds of leather, as shown in Fig-

Fig. 7.9a Ronald R. Roszkiewicz demonstrates how to make a lidded box. Here he is marking the points on the block where the faceplate is to go. Then holes are drilled where the screws are to be placed and the faceplate attached.

Fig. 7.9b The block is screwed onto the head of the lathe and the tool rest is adjusted.

Fig. 7.9c The corners of the block are cut away with a gouge and the piece is roughly shaped into a cylinder.

Fig. 7.9d With a sawtooth machine center bit, a hole is made to accommodate a skew chisel. This process is to start a hole in the lid, which is made backward.

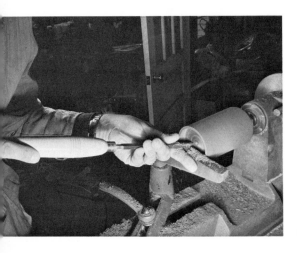

Fig. 7.9e A skew chisel cuts away the interior of the lid to the depth desired.

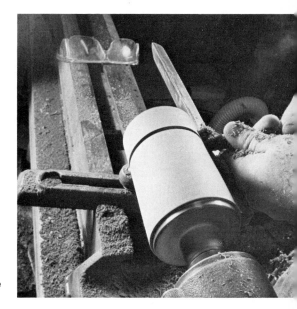

Fig. 7.9f Then a parting tool separates the lid from the body.

Fig. 7.9g The same parting tool is used to cut a lip into the body.

Fig. 7.9h The lid is tested over the body for fit.

Fig. 7.9i Again a sawtooth machine center bit is used to form a hole, this time in the body.

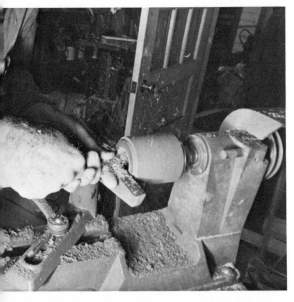

Fig. 7.9j A skew chisel is used to enlarge the hole in the body. Speed at this point is 1700 rpm. The skew chisel is marked so one knows how deeply to cut the opening in the body. A side-cutter chisel is then used to smooth and clean out the sides.

Fig. 7.9k Sanding of the inside is done with #120 open-coat garnet paper.

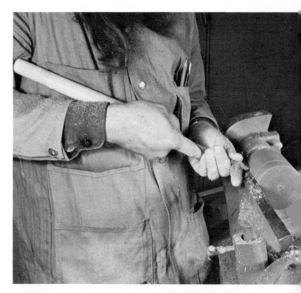

Fig. 7.9l The top is replaced and the form is cleaned up. A round scraper is used, because it is quicker than sandpaper and end grain is difficult to smooth down.

Fig. 7.9m With the lathe rotating all the time, sand with #120 to #220 open-coat garnet paper. The paper has to be moved continuously, otherwise it will burn in—glaze or scratch—the wood.

Fig. 7.9n Then the sanding is followed with #000 or #0000 steel wool. Keep the form rotating.

Fig. 7.9o Ron continues the refining of the finish with teak or rosewood shavings. Because they are oily woods, they help to polish the surface. The machine is then stopped and the surface is oiled with teak oil. If it is done on a rotating lathe, the finish streaks.

Fig. 7.9p Then the piece is parted from the base plate (above the screws) with a parting tool.

Fig. 7.9q Any handy knife is used to cut the last bit off of the base so it doesn't splinter.

Fig. 7.9r The remaining pimple is cut off and the base is oiled, along with a second and third oiling of the whole piece periodically, as the oil is absorbed.

Fig. 7.9s Ron's teakwood container with lid, 5 inches high.

Figs. 7.10, 7.11, and 7.12 Other forms by Ronald R.
Roszkiewicz that have been turned on a lathe.

Fig. 7.13 Turned bowl of Mexican mahogany, 6 inches
high, by James Prestini. *Courtesy: The Museum of
Modern Art Edgar Kaufmann, Jr. Fund*

Fig. 7.14 Turned forms by Joyce Anderson.

Fig. 7.15 A very large (20-inch diameter) flat platter by
Joyce Anderson—a tour de force to avoid warping of
so large and flat a shape.

Fig. 7.16 Charles Gardner's turned cups and platter.

Fig. 7.17 Teak and walnut vases.

Fig. 7.18 Plate and chalice by Mary and Robin Ellis.

ure 7.7l; the base may be covered with felt; holes can be filled with wood filler; or, if enough depth was allowed, the base can be planed and sanded to eliminate the holes.

In the photographic series in Figure 7.9, a craftsman demonstrates the step by step procedures in turning a cylindrical box and matching lid using the faceplate method. Unusual wood forms by a number of different artists, turned by both spindle and faceplate methods, are shown in Figures 7.10 through 7.18.

THE BASICS OF MAKING A CHAIR

Constructing a chair involves the application of many of the skills described earlier in this book. Certainly, chair making is basic to furniture making and a challenge to the evolving woodworker.

The chairs selected to illustrate specific procedures in this chapter are classics: Gimson ladder-backed and spindle-backed chairs and rocker, shown in Figures 8.1, 8.2, and 8.3. Neville Neal of Stockton, England, was an apprentice of Ernest Gimson and is still making Gimson-designed chairs to this day. In the photographic series in this chapter, Mr. Neal demonstrates the classic procedures in chair making. The text and illustrations will provide step by step descriptions for making and assembling individual chair parts, with a detailed discussion of rush work.

CONSTRUCTION PLAN

The usual procedure in constructing a chair is to cut and shape all parts sep-

Fig. 8.1 Basic, ladder-backed Gimson chair by Neville
Neal.

Fig. 8.2 Two Gimson ladder-backed chairs, made of elm wood by Neville Neal.

arately, following a prototype or accurate drawing, then to put all the parts together. Usually the front and back frames are assembled first. Then the side rails are connected. In the case of a rush seat, the arm rests are attached after the rush work has been completed.

Based on these guidelines, you must first plan the type of chair you will make, its dimensions and specifications, then the order in which you plan to make the parts. Review your plan carefully to be certain you have considered every aspect of the design and ensured that all parts will fit accurately.

Joints Traditional chairs normally were constructed with mortise and tenon joints, primarily because dowel joints required pegs to be hand shaped and

Fig. 8.3 A spindle-backed rocking chair by Neville
Neal. *Courtesy: Neville Neal; Copyright: Ruval Industries Bureau*

Fig. 8.4 Neville Neal stores roughly cut and bent parts for chairs on a rack until they are needed.

boring bits were none too precise. Today, chair framing relies more on doweled joints. Certainly, the Gimson chairs are an example of this, as all the attachments are made with doweling.

Materials Ash, which is a quick drying wood (and local to England) is used to make these chairs (*see* Ch. 1, *Common Woods,* for other suitable furniture woods). Ash does not have to be seasoned very long: a few weeks should be adequate (Fig. 8.4). The wood is used in various stages of greenness, because when parts are put together while slightly green, shrinkage will hold them together. Of all the parts used in making the Gimson chairs—arms, chair rails, legs, and slats—the slats are allowed to dry longest.

FORMING PARTS

Bending Back Slats Back slats for a chair, such as the ones in Figures 8.1 and 8.2, are rough cut on a band saw to general proportions before being submitted to the bending operation. The side that will become the inner side of the curve is surfaced, which reduces the danger of excessive compression.

When wood is both wet and hot, its plasticity is increased. The usual practice is to steam wood in a steam box using wet steam, or to submerge the wood in hot or boiling water. Either method works. In the series in Figure 8.5, the wood is boiled. The steaming or soaking time usually takes about one hour per inch of thickness. Green wood can be heated more rapidly than dry

Fig. 8.5a This is an electric device for heating water used to bend wood.

Fig. 8.5b After the wood for the chair slats has been boiled in plain hot water, it is left in the frame for a week, or until dry and the slats become loose. Then they are removed and shaped.

Fig. 8.5c Mr. Neal traces around a template to establish the shape. Then the outline is cut on a band saw.

wood and is easier to bend. Oversteaming or overboiling is undesirable because the mechanical properties of the wood may be impaired by excessive heating; cracking could result when bending wood that is too dry.

After the wood has been softened, the piece should be bent to shape as quickly as possible to minimize the loss of heat and moisture from the inner and outer surfaces. As the wood cools, it loses its plasticity. Mild bends, as in chair slats, can be made over frames or forms without using a tension strap, which is standard procedure where extreme bends are required. Woods will generally bend 1–2 percent without failure; Table K shows the relative rate of success in bending woods.

To fix a bend permanently, the wood must be allowed to cool and dry while in the mold. Cooling and drying causes the wood to lose its plasticity and to become stiff. In the case of the Gimson

Table K. Comparative Bending Breakage of Hardwoods

(Percent of Failure)

Oak, white	9	Ash	36	Maple, hard	51
Oak, red	14	Beech	40	Tupelo	53
Oak, chestnut	18	Gum, red and		Gum, black	66
Magnolia	18	sap	44	Cottonwood	69
Birch, sweet	22	Maple, soft	47	Sycamore	84
Elm, soft	28	Chestnut	50	Basswood	95
		Poplar, yellow	51		

From Donald G. Coleman, "Properties, Selection, and Suitability of Woods for Woodworking," Forest Products Laboratory, Forest Service, U.S. Department of Agriculture

Note: Most hardwoods can be bent readily into a curved form. The comparative low toughness of softwoods as a group makes them difficult to bend without excessive breakage.

chair, the slats are left in the forming frame for about a week, if the weather is dry. When they become loose, they are removed.

Shaping Rails, Legs, or Slats While the back chair legs are sometimes formed by heat bending, as are the slats, chair rails and front legs are always shaped. The slats must also be shaped after drying, since they were only rough cut before bending—they can be shaped on a shave horse, using a draw knife and spoke shaver. This shaping procedure is shown for chair rails in the series in Figure 8.6.

The shave horse is a traditional woodworking bench. The woodworker's feet

Fig. 8.6a Roughly cut seat rails of elm for chairs, to be shaped on a shave horse.

Fig. 8.6b A draw knife is used to shape the wood strips, using foot pressure to hold the wood firmly in place on the shave horse. The draw knife is pulled toward the body and is ideal for this type of operation.

Fig. 8.6c A spoke shaver, which is operated the same way as a drawing knife, is then employed for finer finishing. A piece of a rubber inner tube wrapped around the bar keeps the wood from slipping.

Fig. 8.6d Surface finishing is accomplished on a drum sander.

apply pressure on a bar (wrapped with part of a rubber tire to keep the wood from slipping), which in turn holds the wood in place while work ensues. Meanwhile, in a counter action, a draw knife is used to roughly shape the wood by cutting off excess while the blade is pulled toward the body. A spoke shaver, which is operated the same way as a draw knife, is then employed for finer finishing.

Chair arms and rocker parts are cut on a band saw, following the outlines of a drawn line traced around a template. Refinements are then made by hand finishing these pieces on the shave horse.

Turning Spindles, Legs, or Rails

Chair rails or front legs can be turned on a lathe. The photographic series in Figure 8.7 shows spindles for the back of the Gimson rocker (Fig. 8.3) being spindle turned on a lathe. However, the same technique is used for legs or other cylindrical parts.

ASSEMBLING PARTS

After all parts have been shaped by turning, band saw cutting, or shave horse work, then sanded, they are ready for assembling.

Holes are drilled in the frame parts of

Fig. 8.7a Wood strips are spindle turned on a lathe to create legs and other chair parts. Here a piece is being attached between centers.

Fig. 8.7b A template with pins in it is used to mark the cylinder of wood.

Fig. 8.7c Markings are gauged against a model or prototype, particularly when parts have to be accurately matched.

Fig. 8.7d With a gouge, the spindle is cut to duplicate the model.

Fig. 8.7e The spindle is calibrated for proper thickness, then sanded smooth.

the chair to accept the dowels and back slats. A pva glue called Evo-Stik (it's an English product; the American equivalent is Tite-Bond) is used to glue joints. Neville Neal talks about the old glue pot before the use of modern glues; with the availability of pva glues, work is much easier. Just dip the brush into the glue and apply it.

The back of the chair and the front are assembled and clamped separately. When the glue on these parts has dried, the sides are joined and the whole is clamped together (Fig. 8.8). The arms don't go on until the seat has been woven with rushing, otherwise the arms will interfere with your work.

Finishing Of course, along the way, as parts are refined to their final contours, the wood surfaces are sanded. After all the parts are assembled and glued, the

Fig. 8.8a Joints are glued up after all parts have been made. The back and front are clamped together . . .

Fig. 8.8b . . . then the sides are clamped, with a bit of pulling and pressing to square up all parts of the chair.

chair is dusted free of wood dust and then a protective finish is applied.

Traditionally and today, a mixture of beeswax diluted in turpentine is rubbed on, allowed to be absorbed into the wood, then is buffed to a dull shine with a woolen cloth. This old coating is still used today, although sometimes polyurethane is employed where a harder finish is desired.

RUSH WORK

Rush is a river grass that has been dried after picking so that it does not mildew. Rush as a seating material dates back at least 3,000 years. Stools and chairs with rush seats were found among the possessions of ancient Egyptian kings. Then, the possession of a chair was a sign of high rank. Rush seating became a very popular material in England in the seventeenth century. Most of these seventeenth-century chairs, much like the Gimson chairs, were simple ladder-backed or spindle-backed chairs.

To use the rush, it must be moistened by first soaking the rushes in cold water for 10 minutes, then laying the pieces to be used on and under a water wet bed of burlap for 24 hours. The rushes should be soft and pliable.

Several pieces of rush are worked together at one time. When you are working the top of the seat where the rush will show, you must twist the pieces together. Twisting the rush for the underneath part which will not show is not necessary. The number of pieces twisted together is determined by the thickness of the grass and the overall

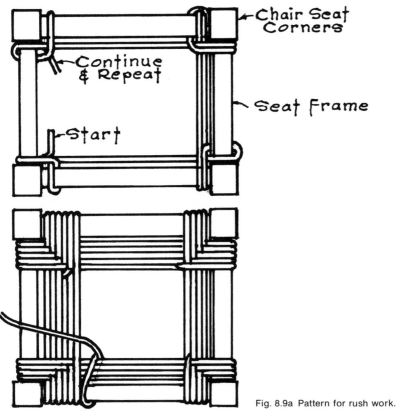

Fig. 8.9a Pattern for rush work.

Fig. 8.9b Rushing for seating is woven under and over, from corner to corner, around the seat frame.

Fig. 8.9c Ends of rushing are tied with a square knot and buried under the seat . . .

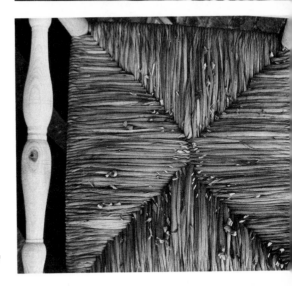

Fig. 8.9d . . . as shown in this view of the underside of the chair.

coarseness or texture desired. After the rushes have been twisted together, the weaving is started by using the thick ends first, with the thin end trailing. The rush should be twisted in the direction away from the worker. When attaching new strands of rush, tie them together—preferably on the underside of the seat—using a square knot or reef knot. Sometimes pieces are just twisted together.

The diagrams and photographs in Figure 8.9 describe the process. To begin, start at one corner of the seat frame. Pulling the rushes tautly, lay a

Figs. 8.10 and 8.11 Two views of a hand-carved walnut chair, 33 inches high, by the Rochester Folk Art Guild. *Courtesy: Rochester Folk Art Guild*

strand of rush over the front bar, then pass the rush under the frame and then up and around the left bar, tightly securing loose ends and keeping the rush tightly packed. The process, as seen in the diagrams, is essentially weaving of the rush fibers under and over the chair frame, moving from corner to corner, until the entire chair seat has been filled. The last end of rush is knotted around one of the rushes under the seat.

A fine example of a hand-carved chair made entirely of wood is shown in Figures 8.10 and 8.11.

MAKING A BASIC CABINET

Cabinetmaking is the synthesis of all the basic skills and knowledge about working with wood. Starting with drawings and plans, the woodworker lists the basic stock needs, along with dimensions. Almost all the hand and hand-controlled machine tools are brought into use. Many of the ways of joining wood are incorporated in a basic cabinet. Methods have to be worked out for doors and drawers to open and close. And, of course, final finishing, that may or may not include handmade or com-mercially made hardware, provides the ultimate flourish to a piece of good design and craftsmanship.

PLANNING THE CABINET

Design Considerations The construction of a cabinet must be basically sound. This means that drawers open and close easily, and that doors open and close without binding. The hidden aspect here is that the *carcass,* which is the framework or the base structure of a cabinet, does not distort. With pulling, pushing, lifting, or other forces applied when opening and closing parts, the frame should not warp or change shape. Overall stiffness and squareness must be maintained.

Positioning of joints, hinges, and pulls; the proportion of a whole to its parts; proportions of parts, such as panels in frames; arrangements and groupings of drawers and doors: all are design considerations.

The design is inextricably tied to subtle considerations such as wood qualities—shrinkage and soundness of structure—as well as to the more obvious aspects of function—proportion and arrangement of parts, kinds of joints and where they show, colors and grains of wood, and so on.

Types of Construction There are three popular ways to construct a cabinet (with variations and modifications of these, as well). A cabinet can be made with solid stock, by using plywood or other sheet material, or by frame and panel construction. The cabinet illustrated here in-the-making combines both solid stock and frame and panel construction, with the carcass made of solid stock and the back panel constructed of a frame and panel.

Consider that a carcass is an open-faced rectangle or square with a fixed back. A force applied to the box will eventually twist the faces of the box, so methods have to be used to prevent twisting in order for the squareness of

the opening to be maintained. Reinforcements have to be designed into the box.

Frame and panel construction is one way to stiffen a carcass—as shown in the back panel of the cabinet being made in the illustrations in this chapter. Increasing the thickness of panels is another method; using cross ribs is still another; interior bracing with cross rails or divisions is representative of many possibilities.

Materials Another design consideration is that shrinkage of the wood has to be taken into account. If the carcass is built with solid wood, then grain direction has to be continuous. This means that side grains are vertical, and that top and bottom grains are parallel to the leading edges. In this case, all the shrinkage would occur across the width of the wood. On the other hand, if one part were horizontal and another part vertical, shrinkage would reduce dimensions differently, thereby locking in or jamming drawers and doors.

Solid wood and plywood should not be mixed indiscriminantly, because each has different shrinkage values. The shrinkage, however, in using solid wood rails or supports for plywood is minimal and would not affect the soundness of construction.

Joints The kinds of joints used should also be considered when designing a cabinet. Dovetails are standard for drawers or parts requiring a pulling action. Drawer runners may be tenoned into the front rail or attached with some kind of mechanical fastener, such as screws, to solid wood sides.

Tops may be joined by mitering and feathering the joint with thru or half-blind (secret) dovetailing, as well as many other ways. Mortise and tenon joints can be used to attach panels to frames.

MAKING THE PARTS

The first procedure involves creating a design and establishing proportions and accurate dimensions, as I have just discussed. These are then translated into a list for the purpose of purchasing lumber and accessory parts. When all materials are on hand, actual woodworking operations begin.

Cutting the Lumber The lumber is first cut to general sizes in all dimensions—thickness, length, and width (Fig. 9.1). The back panel, door, dividers, and drawer parts are cut slightly larger than the final pieces are to be, so that refinements in fitting can be made.

The carcass is cut to exact size.

Forming Joints After the initial cutting of all parts, dovetail joints are cut in the four pieces that will form the carcass, as shown in Figure 9.2. This is followed by cutting mortise joints in the pieces that will form the door (Fig. 9.3).

The frame for the back panel is constructed next, with tenon joints cut to allow for the insertion of interior panels (Fig. 9.4). With carcass, door, and back

Figs. 9.1a, b, and c Lumber is brought down to approximate dimensions in width, length, and depth through use of a band saw. If the cabinet were to be larger, then a table saw would have been appropriate for some of the cutting. Certainly, everything done by machines can also be done by hand.

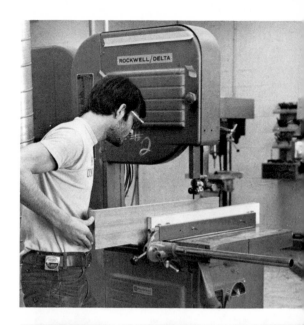

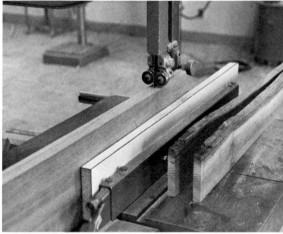

Fig. 9.2a When all parts have been cut for the carcass, joints are formed. Here a marking gauge is used to mark off the depth for a dovetail joint.

Fig. 9.2b The plan for the dovetail joint design is drawn on *all* edges of the carcass corners. Areas to be cut away are darkened so that there is no confusion later as to which areas are to be removed.

Fig. 9.2c Angles are marked with a dovetail marking jig, as shown. A dovetail saw is then used to cut and a chisel to chop out wood across the grain, as shown in *e*, *f*, and *g* parts of this figure.

Fig. 9.2d Tails are marked next, using the previously cut pins as a guide.

Fig. 9.2e Downward cuts are made here, following the proper angles.

Figs. 9.2f and g The negative spaces (marked by X) are chiseled away.

Fig. 9.2h Edges are chamfered with a file.

Fig. 9.2i Carcass parts are only partially tested for fit. Dovetail joints are not made to come apart once they are put together, so full fitting has to wait for the moment of gluing.

Figs. 9.3a and b Next the mortise is cut for the spline with a table saw.

Fig. 9.3c And using a band saw, corner joints are cut as seen in . . .

Fig. 9.3d . . . these results.

Fig. 9.4a A knife is used to mark the position of the middle lap joint in the back panel frame.

Fig. 9.4b The designated area is cut away with a chisel.

Fig. 9.4c Now a groove is cut in the back panel frame with a scraper-cutter to make a tongue for the interior back panels.

Figs. 9.4d and e The fit of the tongue-and-grooved back frame and panel, and the corner joints, is tested before gluing the parts together.

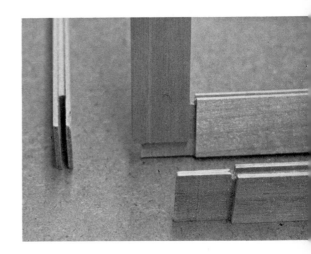

panel joints cut and ready to assemble, you're ready to work on the interior drawers.

The drawer pieces have been previously cut with extra wood left on the sides so that they can be later sanded to fit. Now the half-blind dovetails are cut in the drawer pieces (Fig. 9.5).

Fittings Drawer runners are attached to the sides of the carcass by grooving slots in the carcass to accommodate the runner strips, then gluing and screwing the runners into place (Fig. 9.6).

Then comes the forming of accessories, such as hinges and a door latch—in this case made of wood. Pegs are shaped by pulling and drawing wood through successively smaller holes in a metal plate. Final shaping of the pegs is achieved with a file.

Fig. 9.5a To make the half-blind dovetail joints, mark the depth of the cut, both on the end grain and the edge, with a marking gauge. Then use a dovetail saw to carefully saw down with the grain. Be extremely careful not to slice off the thin strip to be left along the front edge.

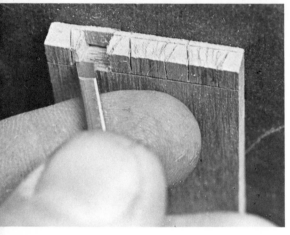

Fig. 9.5b A stop cut is chiseled and then pieces are cut away. The edge that remains to hide the joint will become the front of the drawer. All drawer parts are thus readied for assembly.

ASSEMBLING COMPONENTS

Preliminary Checking The final assembly of the various components is at hand. Before this happens, however, along the way there have been some "dry runs" to test fit. Preliminary estimating as to how well parts fit has been made with caution. There is no objection to fully assembling tenons, without glue of course, to check fit, but dovetails can only be entered halfway as they are not made to come apart. The final dowels should not be forced into place. Use substitute dowels instead, ones that are considerably thinner.

Fig. 9.6a Drawer slides are cut, shaped, and sanded. Areas in the sides of the carcass (the cheeks) are chiseled away to accommodate a partial recessing of the drawer slides. Then holes are drilled for screws and the drawer slides are glued and screwed into place.

Fig. 9.6b Although our cabinet is not yet assembled, as is the one shown here, this side view of the drawers illustrates how they are grooved to slide on the drawer rails.

All joints should be carefully marked so that it is clear which dovetail was made for a particular drawer, for instance. Numbering on the face helps. Even carcass cheeks (vertical side pieces) have a way of transposing themselves.

The Carcass and Back Panel One of the first parts to be attached perma-

nently are the drawer runners to the carcass cheeks (*see* Fig. 9.6). Small holes should be drilled in the runners to keep screws from splitting the wood. Then the runners can be glued, fitted to the carcass in their grooves, and screwed into place.

Next, the carcass joints are glued and joined (Fig. 9.7). Clamps have been adjusted and are ready to attach immedi-

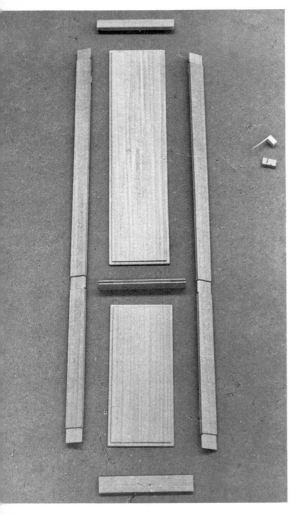

Fig. 9.7a At this point, the carcass is ready to be assembled. Here is a view of the pieces for the back panel, which will be attached to the carcass—after the carcass dovetail joints have been glued and permanently joined.

Fig. 9.7b After the pieces for the back panel are assembled and glued, they are clamped. Note the use of protective pieces of wood under the spring clamps to keep from marking the wood.

ately after glue has been applied. Every part to be joined must be glued thoroughly and excess glue wiped away with a clean damp cloth.

Actual assembly of the carcass should be done on a clean, level foundation. After assembly and before clamping, corners should be checked for squareness. Sometimes a mallet blow will help adjust minor misalignment. After clamping, recheck for squareness at every angle.

The back panel is then put together with glue and reinforced through the tenon with dowels (*see* Fig. 9.7).

Dividers and Drawers The dividers or shelves above the drawers are added now. When clamping, check for bowing in the center of a long span and adjust tension to make certain corners remain square. When you have affirmed that all corners are square and walls are straight, the piece should remain undisturbed until the glue has set. While the carcass, with dividers in place, is drying, the drawers are assembled in the same manner as the carcass (Fig. 9.8). By the time the glue on these joints has thoroughly dried, you will have fitted the hinges and latch into the carcass base.

Accessories Handmade wooden hinges are recessed into the top and bottom sections of the carcass, as shown in Figure 9.9; the fitting is executed by chiseling away the contours needed. The latch is affixed (Fig. 9.10) and the door is now attached. The latch mechanism is covered and hidden with a piece of veneer.

Pegs now are fitted and glued into holes in the carcass cheeks; these can

Fig. 9.8 With the carcass assembled and drawers glued together, all the rest of the parts are ready for attachment. Here they are arrayed.

Fig. 9.9a This is an enlarged picture of the carved wood hinge that is . . .

Fig. 9.9b . . . recessed into the top and bottom sections of the carcass to hold the door. Gluing and screws are used to permanently fix the arms of the hinge.

Fig. 9.10 This is a greatly enlarged view of the door latch, which is hidden from view by being recessed in a cavity in the bottom of the carcass and covered with a piece of veneer.

Fig. 9.11a Finishing touches are performed. Edges of the drawers are chamfered with a file, as shown here.

Fig. 9.11b The drawers are planed to fit into the cabinet without binding.

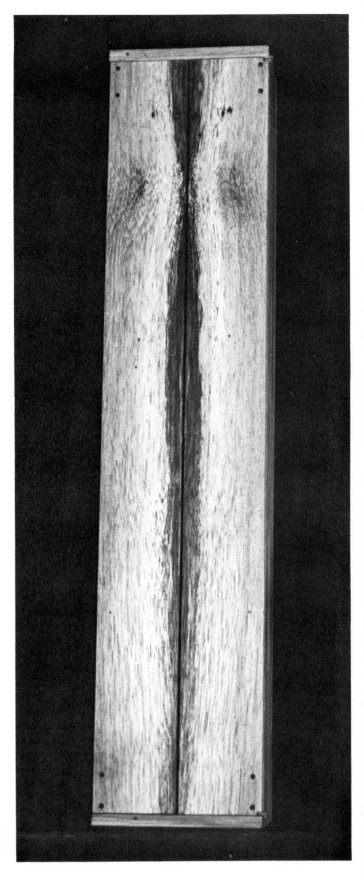

Fig. 9.12 With the drawers, pegs, hinges, latch, and door in place, the cabinet is oiled. The door and carcass are made of hickory. The pattern on the door is a natural effect. *Cabinet by Robert Sperber*

Fig. 9.13 The interior of the jewelry cabinet is of blue cottonwood, which is soft. The pegs, hinges, pins, and lock mechanism are of Honduran rosewood, which is very dense. The finished cabinet is 20 inches high, 7 inches wide, and 5 inches deep.

Fig. 9.14 The back frame and panel show two insets
for hanging the cabinet.

Fig. 9.15 The bottom of the cabinet, with chamfered dovetail joints, the dowel that operates the hinge mechanism, and dowels that plug the screw holes for the hinge. *Photos by Robert Sperber. Cabinet by Robert Sperber*

be used for hanging small items, such as trinkets.

After the drawers have set, clamps are removed and they can be fitted into the carcass by planing and sanding to make slight adjustments (Fig. 9.11). With the drawers in place, final finishing completes this cabinet, designed and made by Robert Sperber (Figs. 9.12 through 9.15).

GLOSSARY

Annual Ring—The layer of wood, consisting of many cells, formed around a tree stem during a single growing season. It is seen most easily in cross section.

Bark—All the material on the outside of the cambium, formed by the cambium.

Bas Relief Carving—Carving in high relief, just short of carving in-the-round, where forms project away from a background.

Bast or Phloem—Inner bark of a tree.

Bending—Softening wood with moisture and heat to increase its plasticity, so its shape can be changed by bending. The bent shape is dried and, in drying, assumes its new form.

Bevel—Cutting or sloping an edge or surface of wood to an oblique angle

Board foot—Standard unit of measure for solid lumber: thickness × width × length, divided by 144.

Bosting—In wood carving, the original rough shaping of actual design elements.

Caliper—Hinged, two-legged instrument used for making and transferring measurements.

Cambium—The layer of actively dividing cells which produces wood cells on the side toward the pith, and bark cells on the side away from the pith.

Carcass (carcase)—The framework or base structure of a cabinet.

Carcass Cheeks—The vertical side panels of a carcass.

Carving—Process of subtracting or cutting away parts of wood, resulting in a form or design.

Chamfering—Cutting of a slight bevel along edges.

Check—Crack or split in wood caused by stress or improper seasoning.

Chip Carving—A variation of low relief carving whereby wedge-shaped pieces are cut out of the wood. The deepest part of the chip is at the apex of the triangle and the most shallow portion is nearest the surface.

Chisel—Tool having a single, beveled cutting edge at one end; driven by hand or by tapping on the handle with a mallet.

Clamp (_cramp_ in England)—A device made of metal or wood, used to hold wood to a rigid surface or rigid while woodworking operations are in process.

Cross Section—The wood surface exposed when a tree stem is cut horizontally and the majority of the cells are cut transversely.

Crosscut—Cutting a log across the grain or in opposition to its fibrous structure.

Direct Carving—Carving in three dimensions.

Dowel—Cylindrical wood rod used to join two pieces of wood, as in joints, or used as elements in a wood design.

Dressed Board—A length of wood that has been seasoned and then planed on all sides.

End Grain Pattern—A pattern in wood resulting from a horizontal cut across a log that shows portions of the ring, pith, heartwood, and sapwood.

Face Grain Pattern—A pattern evident on the face or length of a dressed board.

Faceplate Turning—Wood is fastened to a faceplate, then shaped by tools as the wood revolves on the end of a lathe.

Figure—Any design or distinctive markings that appear on the surface of a piece of wood.

File—A metal cutting tool with ridges, used to abrade wood.

Finishing—The act of sanding the surface of wood with sandpaper or steel wool until the surface is smooth and/or applying a protective material such as oil, wax, or resin to the surface to prevent loss of or acquisition of moisture.

Gouges—Metal cutting tools, shaped in cross section from a variety of Us to Vs, and used to cut away or carve wood.

Grain—The fibrous structure of wood that is displayed as a pattern.

Grain Direction—Direction parallel to the long axis of the majority of cells in a piece of wood.

Green Wood—Unseasoned wood before drying process.

Hardwood—Wood from a broad-leaved tree, characterized by the presence of vessels, e.g., oak, ash, or birch.

Heartwood—The older, harder, inner part of the stem which, in the growing tree, no longer contains living cells. It is generally darker than sapwood, though the boundary is not always distinct.

Incise Carving—The cutting of incisions or grooves into the surface of wood.

Joints—Various ways two or more pieces of wood are put together. Some examples are butt joints, doweling, dovetailing, tongue and groove, and so on.

Kerf—Path cut through wood by saw blade.

Laminating—Gluing together several layers of wood in sandwich form.

Lignin—An amorphous substance which infiltrates and surrounds the cellulose strands in wood, binding them together to give a strong mechanical structure. It amounts to 15 to 30 percent by weight of the wood substance.

Low Relief Carving—Cutting away, in a shallow depth, of the background, leaving the foreground in slight relief, sometimes with some modeling or shaping of the foreground elements.

Mallet—A hardwood, hammerlike tool, used to drive chisels or gouges into wood.

Miter—Bevel wood pieces to match together at a corner.

Miter Box—Device for guiding a saw at the proper angle for making a miter joint.

Monolyxous—Carving a form from a solid piece of wood, when woods are not laminated together or parts joined.

Plugging—Technique of placing a wood peg over a screw to hide the presence of the screw.

Plywood—A series of thin layers of wood, glued together to form a solid sheet. The grain direction runs at right angles in adjacent layers.

Rasp—A metal tool much like a file that has rough, burrlike surface used to abrade wood.

Riffles—Small files or rasps with curved ends.

Rough Out—Making undetailed, rough cuts to approximate final shape in woodcarving.

Rough-sawn Wood—Wood boards cut from a log, before dressing.

Rush Work—The wrapping or weaving of rush or river grass to form a chair seat.

Sapwood—Wood immediately inside the cambium of the living tree, containing living cells and reserve materials, and in which most of the upward water movement takes place. More permeable and less durable than the heartwood to which it is ultimately converted.

Seasoning—The drying of wood to eliminate most of its moisture content.

Softwood—Wood from a coniferous or cone-bearing tree, characterized by the absence of vessels, e.g., fir, pine, spruce.

Spindle Turning—A length of wood turned between a moving (live) center or element and stationary (dead) center on a lathe.

Staining—Coloring of wood with pigment that permits the grain to show through.

Stop Cuts—Cutting vertically into a wood surface to outline and provide protection against cutting too far in diagonal or horizontal cutting.

Template—Pattern or shape that becomes a guide, from which outlines are traced onto the wood.

Try Square—Instrument consisting of two straight edges secured at right angles to each other; used to lay off right angles and test squareness of work.

Undercut—Cutting back beneath an area when carving.

Veneer—A thin slice of wood cut with a knife or saw from a log.

Warpage—Tendency of wood to twist or curve out of shape as a result of uneven drying or exposure to moisture.

Whittling—Carving in three dimensions of forms that can be held by hand.

Adhesives

Most lumber supply sources such as local lumber yards, building supply stores, and hardware stores sell Weldwood, Titebond, Liquid Hide Glue, Elmer's Glue, and other plastic resin glues.

Finishes

H. Behlen & Bros., Inc.
P.O. Box 698
Amsterdam, NY 12010

Everything for wood finishing.

Gaston Wood Finishes
3630 East 10th Street
Bloomington, IN 47401

All types of finishes and finishing accessories, such as Tack-Cloth, sandpaper, brushes, solvents, and thinners

Minwax Company, Inc.
72 Oak Street
Clifton, NJ 07014

Oil finishes and transparent oil stains

Rustins Ltd.
Waterloo Road
Cricklewood, London NW2
England

A remarkable clear plastic, plus other fine finishes

Woodcraft Supply Corp.
313 Montvale Avenue
Woburn, MA 01801

Wood finishes, such as Watco Danish Oil

Hardware

Albert Constantine & Son, Inc.
2050 Eastchester Road
Bronx, NY 10461

Drawer and door pulls, locks, brackets, hinges, glides, and casters

Craftsman Wood Service Co.
2727 South Mary Street
Chicago, IL 60608

Drawer and door slides and tracks, hinges, locks, screws, casters, guides, door and drawer pulls

William Hunrath Co., Inc.
153 East 57th Street
New York, NY 10022

Hinges, drawer and door pulls, casters

Tremont Nail Co.
11 Elm Street
Wareham, MA 02571

Old-fashioned cut nails

Tools and Machinery

Abbey Materials Corp.
116 West 29th Street
New York, NY 10001

Assorted files, accessories, and power tools

American Machine and Tool Co. Fourth and Spring Streets Royersford, PA 19468	Low-priced machinery and power tools
Black and Decker Towson, MD 21204	Power tools and accessories
Buck Bros., Inc. Millbury, MA	Woodcarving tools
Colbert Industries 10107 Adella Avenue South Gate, CA 90280	Panavise—various kinds of vises
Albert Constantine & Son, Inc. 2050 Eastchester Road Bronx, NY 10461	Tools for veneer work and upholstery work
Craftsman Wood Service Co. 2727 South Mary Street Chicago, IL 60608	Power tools and accessories, hand tools, carving tools
Dremel Manufacturing Division 4915 21st Street Racine, WI 53406	Moto-Lathe, Moto-Shop, Moto-Tool, variable speed controls, foot pedal, accessories
Force Machinery Co. 2271 Route 22 Union, NJ 07083	Retail general supplier
Garrett Wade Co. 302 Fifth Avenue New York, NY 10001	Carving and clamping tools and accessories
Leichtung & Galmitz, Inc. 187 Mayfield Road Cleveland, OH 44124	Woodcarving and wood-turning tools
The Luxite Corp. 85 Liberty Street Jersey City, NJ 07306	Saw blades
Parry & Son Ltd. 325/329 & 333 Old Street Shoreditch, London EC1 England	Full range of power tools and accessories, machinery, and hand tools
Rockwell International 400 North Lexington Avenue Pittsburgh, PA 15208	Power tools, industrial machinery
Rockwell International of Canada, Ltd. 40 Wellington St. P.O. Box 848 Guelph, Ontario N1H 6M7	Power tools, industrial machinery
Sculpture Associates 114 East 25th Street New York, NY 10010	Woodcarving and power tools and accessories

Sculpture Services, Inc. 9 East 19th Street New York, NY 10003	Carving tools and hand tools
Severance Tool Industries 3790 Orange P.O. Box 1866 Saginaw, MI 48605	Rotary files and burrs
Stanley Tools New Britain, CT 06050	Full range of hand tools
The Stanley Tool Works of Canada, Ltd. P.O. Box 3001, Station B Hamilton, Ontario	Full range of hand tools
L. S. Starrett Co. Athol, MA 01331	Complete line of measuring tools and precision instruments
Tashiro Hardware Co. 109–113 Prefontaine Place Seattle, WA 98104	Japanese hand tools
Alec Tiranti, Ltd. 70 High Street Theale, Berkshire England	Woodcarving tools, wood-turning tools, and assorted hand tools, such as files and rifflers
Tool AG Lohwiestrasse 28 CH-8123 Ebmatingen Zurich, Switzerland	Power tools
Tools Unlimited, Inc. P.O. Box 7 Brentwood, NY 11717	Power tools and machinery
Woodcraft Supply Corp. 313 Montvale Avenue Woburn, MA 01801	Full range of hand tools, accessories, and carving tools

Wood

The yellow pages of your local directory will yield lumber supply sources. A phone call to one will tell you where to find hardwoods, veneers, etc.

Albert Constantine & Son, Inc. 2050 Eastchester Road Bronx, NY 10461	Veneers
Craftsman Wood Service 2727 South Mary Street Chicago, IL 60608	Veneers, moldings, hardwoods, plywoods

Designers Resource Group Box 142 Seabrook, TX 77565	Massive cubes and cylinders of sculpting woods
Elwilply Veneer Co., Ltd. 48A Eagle Whard Road N.1 London, England	Veneers
Paul K. Guillow, Inc. Wakefield, MA 01880	Balsa wood
W. W. Howard Bros., Ltd. Howard House Lanrick Road Poplar, London E. 14 OJF England	Veneers, hardwood, plywood
M & M Hardwood 5344 Vineland Avenue North Hollywood, CA 91601	Hardwoods, veneers, edgings and trims, moldings
Neill & Spanjer Fairfield Avenue & Market St. Kenilworth, NJ	Hardwoods, plywoods, moldings
Sculpture Associates 114 E. 25th Street New York, NY 10010	Wood for carving, sculptures
Sculpture Services, Inc. 9 East 19th Street New York, NY 10003	Wood for carving, sculptures

Bridge, Paul and Crossland, Austin, *Designs in Wood*. New York: Frederick A. Praeger, 1969

Child, Peter, *The Craftsman Woodturner*. London: G. Bell & Sons, 1973

DalFabbro, Marico, *How to Build Modern Furniture*. New York: McGraw Hill, 1957

Dryad Press, *Cane and Rush Seating*. New York: Alnap

Edlin, Herbert L., *What Wood is That?* New York: Viking Press, 1969

Feirer, John L., *Cabinetmaking and Millwork*. Peoria, Ill: Charles A. Bennett, 1970

Hayward, Charles H., *Woodwork Joints*. New York: Drake, 1974

Hayward, Charles H., *Practical Veneering*. London: Evans Brothers, 1971

Hennessey, James and Papanek, Victor, *Nomadic Furniture*. New York: Pantheon, 1973

Heelas, Edgar H., *Craftwork in Wood*. London: Oxford U. Press, 1940

Hinckley, F. Lewis, *Directory of Historic Cabinet Woods*. New York: Bonanza, MCMLX

Joyce, Ernest, *The Encyclopedia of Furniture Making*. New York: Drake, 1970

Laury, Jean Ray, *Wood Applique*. New York: Van Nostrand Reinhold, 1973

Mason, Bernard S., *Woodcraft*. New York: Barnes & Noble, 1974

Meilach, Dona Z., *Contemporary Art in Wood*. New York: Crown, 1968

Neelands, R. W., *Important Trees of Eastern Forests*. Southern Region, Atlanta: USDA, Forest Service, 1968

Nilsson, Ake R., *Woodware*. London: Mills & Boon, 1972

Rich, Jack C., *Sculpture in Wood*. New York: Oxford U. Press, 1970

Rottger, Ernst, *Creative Wood Design*. New York: Van Nostrand Reinhold, 1960

Sack, Walter, *Woodcarving*. New York: Van Nostrand Reinhold, 1973

Sloane, Eric, *A Museum of Early American Tools*. New York: Ballantine, 1964

Sloane, Eric, *A Reverence for Wood*. New York: Funk & Wagnalls, 1965

Willcox, Donald J., *New Design in Wood*. New York: Van Nostrand Reinhold, 1970

Zanker, Francis D., *Foundation of Design in Wood*. Northgates, Leicester: Dryad Press, 1970

INDEX

Page numbers in *italics* indicate information in illustrations.

Adhesives. *See* Gluing
Age of tree, 6, 218
Anderson, Joyce and Edgar, *55, 99, 145, 148, 178, 179*
Annual ring. *See* Age of tree
Attachment, *63, 76,* 93, *95–98*
Attachment aids. *See* Tools

Barrettes, 125–129, *126–128*
Basic processes. *See* Processes
Bas relief. *See* High relief carving
Bast. *See* Wood
Beehive, Romania, 12
Bending, 12, 24, 41, 45, *56–57,* 186, *187,* 188, 218
Bevel, 218
Blockboard. *See* Laminboard
Board foot, 11
Bosting, 109, 218
Bowls, 24, 41, *149, 167, 168, 177*
Boxes, 41, 68, 79–99, *103–105, 118, 120, 175*
Bury, Pol, *74*

Cabinet, 41, 198–217
Caliper, 218
Cambium. *See* Wood
Carcass, 199, 200, 210, *211, 212, 214,* 217, 218
Carcass cheeks, 218
Carving, 12, 37, 41, 105, *107,* 108–112, 134–151, 218, 219
Carving tools, 29, *110,* 134
Chair, 41
    Gimson, 182–197
Chalice, 181
Chamfering, 89, 204, *213,* 218
Checking of wood. *See* Cracking of wood
Chess set, *13*
Child, Peter, *157, 159, 160, 162–168*
Chip carving, *107,* 112, *115–118,* 218
Chisel, 23, 29, *86, 87, 95, 107,* 110, 115, 141, *203, 206, 208,* 218
Ciscell, Bob, *56–57*
Clamping, 72, *86,* 218
Contours. *See* Templates
Cracking of wood, 8, 9, 218
Crosscut, 218
Cross-section, 218
Curling. *See* Bending

Cutting of wood, 9, 10, 12, 41, 43, *45, 46, 47, 48, 49, 50, 52,* 80, *81, 82, 83,* 93, *94, 95,* 130, 132, *200, 201,* 202

Design, 42, 79, 80, 109, 146, 198–200
Direct carving, 134–147, 218
Dovetail. *See* Joints
Dowel, *92,* 207, 218
Dressed board, 218
Drilling and boring tools. *See* Tools

Earrings, 129–130, *131*
Edge grain. *See* Grain
Ellis, Robin and Mary, *13, 181*
End grain pattern, 218
Environmental conditions, 5
Equipment, 23–40, 221, 222
    lathes, 37, 41, 152, *153, 154*
    sanding machines, 35–37
    vises and clamps, 38–40, 189

Faceplate turning, 154, 162–168, 218
Fastening, 12, 24, 41, *63*
Fesese, Ola, *138*
Figure, 22, 218
File, 213, 218
Finishing, 12, 52, 66, 68, 70, 75, 76, 78, 89, 90, 93, 99, 100, 113, 129, 134, *167, 168, 169, 175,* 192, 193, 218, 221
Fischman, Irving, *70*
Frame and panel, 92, 199
Friedman, Alan, *124*
Furniture, 9

Gagnon, Priscilla, *144, 145*
Gardner, Charles, *179*
Gimson chair. *See* Chair
Gluing, 9, 12, 45, 47, *58, 59,* 65, *71, 72, 112,* 121–125, 192, 221
Gouges, 24, 29, 109, 110, 115, 218
Grading of lumber, 10, 11
Grain, 9, 16, 43, *71,* 109, 218
    vertical, 9
    edge, 9
Grain direction, 218
Green wood. *See* Unseasoned wood

Handsaws. *See* Saws
Hand tools, 23–40
  ease of working with, 18
Hardware, 93, *95*, 198, *212, 213*
Hardwood, 5, 6, 7, 9, 10, 14–22, 219
Heartwood. *See* Wood
Heat and flame, 101–102
High relief carving, 115, 119, 120, 218
Hinges, *95, 96*, 207, 211, *212, 215*
Hostetler, David, *150*
Hot plate, *66, 67, 117*

Incise carving, 219
Insects, 5

Jig, 87, *88*
Joining, 12, 45, 47
Joints, 41, 45, 47, *63, 64, 65,* 66, *69, 70, 76, 77,*
  106, 199, 200, 210, 219
  dovetail, *84–88,* 90, 184, 186, *193,* 199,
  202–204, 208, 217
  mortise and tenon, 200, *204–207*

Kerf, 219
Kiln seasoning. *See* Seasoning
Kinds of woods, 14–18, 153
Knots, 10

Lamination, 41, 121–130, *131–134,* 219
Laminboard, 10
Lamp, *73, 123, 161*
Langlais, Bernard, *75*
Lathe. *See* Turning; Equipment
Leaves, 4, 7
Lignin, 219
Lonning, Kari, *54*
Low relief carving, 109–112, 219
Lumber, 9. *See also* Wood
  grading, 10, 11
  structural, 10
  factory or shop, 10
  blemishes, 10
  purchasing, 11

Machinery. *See* Equipment
Makepeace, John, *8, 56*
Mallet, 23, 40, 115, 219
Marquetry, 11
Measuring, 11, 37, *44*
Measuring devices, 37, *38*
Mirrors, *145, 147*
Miter, 219

Miter box, 219
Monolyxous, 219

Neal, Neville, 182–197
Necklaces, *132, 133, 148*

Odes-Neaderland, Louise, *147*
Opening a box, *94*

Pegs. *See* Dowels
Plain sawed wood, 9
Planing, *82, 83, 84*
Plate, *179, 181*
Plugging, *217,* 219
Plywood, 9, *10, 13,* 199, 219
Power tool carving, 147, 151
Processes, 41–78
  fundamental, 43–47
Purchasing lumber. *See* Lumber
Puzzle making, 43, *52–54*

Quarter sawed wood, 9

Rasp, 100, 219
Raw wood. *See* Unseasoned wood
Riffles, 219
Rings, *134, 148*
Rochester Folk Art Guild, *71, 196, 197*
Roszkiewicz, Ronald R., *169–176*
Rough out, 108, 136, 219
Rough-sawn wood, 219
Rush work, 194, 195, *205–208,* 219

Safety, 27, 51, 108, 151
Sanding, 35–37, *51,* 68, *97, 166, 172,* 173, 190
Sanding machines. *See* Equipment
Sandpaper, 4, 35
Sapwood. *See* Wood
Saws
  handsaws, 24–28
  machine saws, 26–28
Scrap, 54, *71–73,* 75
Sculptures, 24, 45, *57,* 74, 75, *124, 142, 144,*
  150
Seasoning of wood, 8, 9, 219
Sharpening tools. *See* Tool sharpening
Shrinkage, 9, 11, 20, 198, 199
Softwood, 5, 6, 7, 9, 10, 14–22, 219
Spencer, Edwin, 125–134
Sperber, Robert, *81–98, 200–217*
Spindle turning, 154, 158–162, 219
Staining, 219

Stop cuts, *107, 111,* 219
Surface cutting tools. *See* Tools

Templates, 43, *143, 188, 191, 202,* 219
Texturing, 100–107
Tongue and groove. *See* Joints
Tools, 23–40, *44, 45, 46, 47, 48, 49, 50, 51, 52,*
    221, 222
   attachment aids, 40
   drilling and boring, 31–35
   measuring, 37
   surface cutting, 28–31
   woodturning, 37, 41, 153–157
Tool sharpening, 108, *156, 157*
Toys, *71, 76, 77*
Trivet, *64–67*
Try square, 219
Turning, 12, 37, 41, 152–181, 190, *191, 192*

Undercut, 219
Unseasoned wood, 9, 10, 219
Use of tools, 41–52, *44, 45, 64, 65*

Vase, *178, 180*
Veneer, 9, 10, 11, 45, *56–62,* 125, *213,* 219
Vertical grain. *See* Grain
Vises and clamps. *See* Equipment

Warpage, 9, 19, 43, 219
Water. *See* Wood, moisture
Whittling. *See* Carving
Wirkkala, Tapio, *13*
Wood
   age, 5, 6
   bark, 5, 218
   bast, 5, 218
   cambium, 5, 218
   cells, 9
   characteristics or traits, 4, 6, 7, 14–22
   classification, 6, 7, 11, 14, *16*
   functions, 3, 4, 12, 14–18
   growth, 5
   heartwood, 5, 219
   insect enemies, 5
   kinds. *See* Kinds of woods
   moisture, 5, 8, 9, 10, 153
   phloem, 5
   pith, 5
   properties, 3, 8, 12, 19
   sap, 5, 8
   sapwood, 5, 219
   sources, 223, 224
   structure, 4, 5, 9
   trunk, 5
   uses, 10, 14–18

Yu-Lin, Cheng, 112, *146*

Thelma R. Newman, author, artist, educator, has written more than sixteen books on arts and crafts. She received her bachelor's degree from the College of the City of New York, her Master of Arts degree from New York University, and her doctorate from Columbia University, Teacher's College. She studied woodworking at Columbia and with private woodworkers, such as Peter Child in England.

The author has taught at New Jersey State College, North Texas State College, Newark State College, and for four years was director of art for the Union Township, New Jersey, schools.

Thelma Newman has studied woodworking techniques virtually all over the world—in Africa, Southeast Asia, Japan, the Americas, Yugoslavia, Bulgaria, and England. In addition to numerous books in many craft fields, she has also published many articles in technical, art, and learned journals.